PRAISE FOR *BOUNCE BACK*

What a brilliant subject for a book, courageously chosen and boldly tackled. We all fail. What matters is what we do next, how we cope with it. I will still fail, but after reading Susan Kahn's first-rate book I know I can bounce back. And if I can cope more confidently with failure, I'm more likely to succeed.
Daniel Finkelstein, *Times* columnist

Bounce Back: How to fail fast and be resilient at work should be a staple on any entrepreneur's bookshelf. Susan Kahn's book is full of practical advice and tools for anyone trying to understand themselves deeper, become a better leader and coworker, and live a balanced life. Not a book to simply be read, but a manual that also gives its reader space for introspection and questioning.
Courtney Carlsson, Co-Founder and CEO, Paradym

In *Bounce Back*, Susan Kahn provides a comprehensive exploration of our resilience both at work and in our personal lives. Susan skilfully weaves insights from neuroscience, psychoanalysis and positive psychology to create a practical and essential guide to building more resilient behaviours. The book also explores issues of human purpose with the help of Aristotle, Frankl and the Japanese idea of Ikigai, as well as key concepts in leadership (and followership) which explore with kindness and compassion the difficulties that we face leading in the modern world of work. Each chapter finishes with some helpful and readily applicable exercises which can be put into practice straight away by the reader. In short, a thoroughly enjoyable, well-researched and hugely practical book which is essential reading in these uncertain times.
Raul Aparici, coach, consultant and facilitator, and Lead Faculty at The School of Life

Often books like this fall between two types. They are either too to complex and psychological or too quick-fix and simplistic. Dr Susan Kahn has squared that circle by producing a book which mixes real depth and richness with accessible practical advice. There's no better book on resilience that you could read.

Derek Draper, CEO, CDP Leadership Consultants, and author of *Create Space*

This wonderful book by Dr Susan Kahn focuses on what many believe to be the key to success at work – our psychological resilience and our ability to thrive, rather than crumble, in a changing environment. In *Bounce Back*, Kahn refers to numerous sources, both ancient and modern, yet writes in an accessible style, making the reader feel she is there for us, as a generous, supportive coach helping us as we tackle today's workplace challenges. Although the book is aimed at the individual, with lots of thoughtful and insightful exercises, it could enrich teams and entire organizations, boosting both their well-being agenda alongside their commercial success.

Kate Davies, CEO, Notting Hill Genesis

Dr Susan Kahn writes of that most human of dichotomies: our drive to succeed and our fear of failure. It is here that she places resilience, not as a binary construct but something malleable, adaptable, flexible and (importantly) something that can be learned and developed. Powerful exercises bring the material to life, and allow for deeper insights. *Bounce Back* is a deeply compassionate and optimistic work. From Seneca to Emerson, Dickens to Freud, Aristotle to Nietzsche, the book draws on a wide range of thinkers and addresses major issues such as our sense of purpose, who we are and how we can flourish. In a world where our expectations of workplaces, work colleagues, structure, technology, communication, tasks, availability and skill have all been transformed, we are in desperate need for guidance and orientation – which is here in abundance.

Prof Andreas Liefooghe PhD, Director, Operation Centaur, and Founder and CEO, Shrink Technologies

Bounce Back is energizing, and expertly and elegantly written. With well-researched explanations and practical exercises to help the reader reflect and advance, *Bounce Back* will lift you out of 'stuck' and into hopeful and empowered. Every employee should read it. So should their managers and leaders.
Rachel Ellison MBE DUniv, executive leadership coach specializing in global organizations in the private, public and third sectors

Susan Kahn takes us on a journey to better understand how to harness our ability to bounce back. Resilience is a trait to be practiced and developed and reclaimed in our modern world. Easily accessible, her chapters encourage understanding and growth, and dipping into the tasks will create personal development. Her examples encourage us to risk, embrace failure with positivity and bounce back stronger.
Ruth Green, senior counsellor, mentor, trainer and facilitator

Anyone reading *Bounce Back* cannot fail to pick up highly useful strategies for achieving results. It is steeped in carefully thought through, logically assembled suggestions. The writing style is informative, practical and backed with robust references. This self-help book covers a broad range of accessible, easy to implement ideas. There will be more than one that resonates and that can be actioned to achieve impact.
David Goldstone, Managing Partner, Osprey Clarke, and CEO, Pandion International

In this book, Susan Kahn brings together her considerable experience into a crucial yet fun and practical business book. Bouncing back from failure is what makes great entrepreneurs. I have thoroughly enjoyed reading it and doing some of the exercises with my colleagues.
Nathaniel Meyohas, Partner, Blandford Capital

A fantastic insight into becoming stronger and more resilient and enabling people to get the best out of their effort and endeavours in the workplace. A really practical self-help guide to develop one's skills and perspective.
Daniel Kattan, Real Estate Investor, K3Invest

Bounce Back

How to fail fast and be resilient at work

Susan Kahn

KoganPage

Publisher's note

Every possible effort has been made to ensure that the information contained in this book is accurate at the time of going to press, and the publishers and authors cannot accept responsibility for any errors or omissions, however caused. No responsibility for loss or damage occasioned to any person acting, or refraining from action, as a result of the material in this publication can be accepted by the editor, the publisher or the author.

First published in Great Britain and the United States in 2020 by Kogan Page Limited

Apart from any fair dealing for the purposes of research or private study, or criticism or review, as permitted under the Copyright, Designs and Patents Act 1988, this publication may only be reproduced, stored or transmitted, in any form or by any means, with the prior permission in writing of the publishers, or in the case of reprographic reproduction in accordance with the terms and licences issued by the CLA. Enquiries concerning reproduction outside these terms should be sent to the publishers at the undermentioned addresses:

2nd Floor, 45 Gee Street
London
EC1V 3RS
United Kingdom

122 W 27th St, 10th Floor
New York, NY 10001
USA

4737/23 Ansari Road
Daryaganj
New Delhi 110002
India

www.koganpage.com

© Susan Kahn, 2020

The right of Susan Kahn to be identified as the author of this work has been asserted by her in accordance with the Copyright, Designs and Patents Act 1988.

ISBNs

Hardback	978 1 78966 028 9
Paperback	978 0 7494 9736 1
Ebook	978 0 7494 9735 4

British Library Cataloguing-in-Publication Data

A CIP record for this book is available from the British Library.

Library of Congress Cataloging-in-Publication Data

Names: Kahn, Susan (Consultant), author.
Title: Bounce back : how to fail fast and be resilient at work / Susan Kahn.
Description: New York : Kogan Page, 2020. | Includes bibliographical references and index.
Identifiers: LCCN 2019031286 (print) | LCCN 2019031287 (ebook) | ISBN 9780749497361 (paperback) | ISBN 9781789660289 (hardback) | ISBN 9780749497354 (ebook)
Subjects: LCSH: Career development. | Failure (Psychology) | Resilience (Personality trait) | Success.
Classification: LCC HF5381 .K324 2019 (print) | LCC HF5381 (ebook) | DDC 650.1–dc23
LC record available at https://lccn.loc.gov/2019031286
LC ebook record available at https://lccn.loc.gov/2019031287

Typeset by Integra Software Services, Pondicherry
Print production managed by Jellyfish
Printed and bound by CPI Group (UK) Ltd, Croydon, CR0 4YY

For all the vulnerable at work,
you can bounce back.

CONTENTS

ABOUT THE AUTHOR

Dr Susan Kahn is a Business Psychologist: a coach, lecturer, consultant and mediator. A committed lifelong learner, she is the Programme Director for the Postgraduate Coaching Certificate at Birkbeck, University of London, teaching leaders how to coach. Susan is an inaugural member of the Business Faculty at The School of Life, where she teaches and facilitates emotional intelligence in the workplace.

Her coaching work helps executives in diverse sectors perform authentically and effectively. She also works with equine coaching and has appeared on the BBC.

She is a speaker and has lectured at conferences globally as a member of ISPSO, the International Society for the Psychoanalytic Study of Organizations. Susan works as a group relations consultant, exploring and examining group dynamics, particularly those below the surface.

Her first book, *Death and the City*, tackled loss, mourning and melancholia at work and is an examination of the experience of organizational endings during the financial crisis. Her study using psychoanalytic observation as a research tool was awarded a prize by Birkbeck.

Her latest publication, *Bounce Back*, brings her work together. Recognising vulnerability in herself and in others lies at the core of all her work.

She lives in London with her husband, family and very noisy dog.

FOREWORD

This is a timely and relevant book. The world of work is changing rapidly, and many developments are exciting and full of potential. The ability to transform and adapt to the needs of clients and stakeholders is challenging and energizing. But there is also a fear of trying new things, of failing, even of learning.

Recognizing that no matter what your role at work you will face difficulty, you will find yourself unsure, but you will also have the chance to find courage and strength to tackle the unexpected. Resilience is a vital quality at work.

To those who feel that life doesn't get easier or more forgiving this book helps you navigate the impact of failure, adversity and change. This book will give you tools to help you flourish at work, to explore deeply your relationship with failure and to dig below the surface and examine what might be holding you back.

Being able to build and use resilience is not the domain of those with some innate skill. In these pages you will find countless nuggets of advice and many illuminating examples of how you can cultivate resilience and build reserves you can draw on.

Whether a leader or a follower, in times of disruption or stability, when experiencing loss or developing new products, relationships and teams you will be challenged, you may feel vulnerable. As Susan notes:

Work is full of satisfying, challenging and rewarding moments.
It can offer us support, friendship, understanding, learning and development. But work can also be a place where we feel out of our depth, where we question our ability to take on challenges, and may feel inadequate, hurt and depleted. Resilience is therefore essential for us at work, and we need to understand failure, respond to it quickly and build our capacity to bounce back.

But where this breaks new ground is how it conceptualizes the colossal positive and forward-looking capacity unleashed by the confidence that resilience can deliver. From operational challenges, to how to deal with decisions that require some form of reversal. From being prepared to challenge old notions to managing the rollercoaster of technology, being prepared to innovate, to pivot, to lead change and to take on the responsibility for big calls.

One of the mantras I have benefited from in business is the question I ask of the people I work with: 'What would you do if you weren't afraid?' It's a rallying cry to challenge orthodoxy. Never say that you can't do something, or that something seems impossible, or that something can't be done, no matter how discouraging or harrowing it may be. It is our own minds that hold us back and it is here that resilience helps us to chart our own reality. One where you face your future with excitement and energy and can break through any potential self-imposed limitations and raise the opportunities that the power your unleashed mind can create.

This book will have a profound impact on those who read it and take its message to heart. One of not just coping, but of flourishing. One of not just managing risks but of unbound creativity.

The future of work requires us to recognize that if we do what we have always done we will get the results we always have. It is in this work that individuals can find the means to equip our modern economy with the leaders it needs.

Nicola Mendelsohn CBE
VP EMEA Facebook

ACKNOWLEDGEMENTS

For those who have helped me to bounce back, so many times, thank you.

My tribe, Neville, Victoria, Oliver, Charlie and Sam – I'd take a bullet for you.

My critical readers: Rene Anisfeld, Rachel Ellison, Samuel Kahn, Suzanne Ellis-Ferera, Charles Kahn, Neville Kahn, Victoria Tenzer, Oliver Tenzer, Anna Levy, Jeremy Newman.

And for the ring of resilience and support that is constant, my sister Judi Newman.

Dr Andreas Liefooghe, my colleagues and the students at Birkbeck, University of London, and at The School of Life, whom I teach but from whom I learn so much. And to those who provide me space to think and to whom I turn for guidance and wisdom, Dr Sharon Numa and Dr Anton Obholzer.

I would like to thank Rebecca Bush at Kogan Page for bringing the idea of the book to me and for her constant support and insights.

LIST OF EXERCISES

Chapter 4

Chapter 5

Chapter 6

Chapter 7

Chapter 8

Introduction

Work is full of satisfying, challenging and rewarding moments. It can offer us support, friendship, understanding, learning and development. But work can also be a place where we feel out of our depth, where we question our ability to take on challenges, and may feel inadequate, hurt and depleted. Resilience is therefore essential for us at work, and we need to understand failure, respond to it quickly and build our capacity to bounce back.

Resilience can be understood in many ways. There is the image of resilience captured in the tree that can bend slightly in the storm; it can move with the winds and return to its upright position when the storm has passed. In science, resilience is identified as the ability of material to return to its original state after it has been stretched or bent. There are also many physical, emotional and psychological manifestations of resilience. It is a concept that can be applied to a nation's response to a natural disaster; an organization's ability to cope with a merger; a team's ability to cope with the death of their leader; or perhaps an individual who has started a new job away from trusted colleagues, or been able to cope with their ill parents and marriage breakdown and keep working.

What unites all these different expressions of resilience is the ability to *adapt and change* to the circumstances they face. In a Darwinian sense, survival is not necessarily the preserve of the strongest or the most intelligent of the species; it is the preserve of the species that can adjust and modify.

The subject of resilience is important to me personally as well as professionally. As a child I was incredibly shy and awkward. If someone looked at me, never mind spoke to me, I would blush furiously and hate myself for not being able to be confident and calm. I was desperate to please and unbearably self-conscious. Over the years I learnt to observe people and relationships and to develop my capacity to deal with difficulty. I sought help, gathered trusted friends and advisors and became competent at doing things that would have been unimaginable to my younger self. I now consult, lecture, coach and mediate with confidence, but always with an awareness of the potential vulnerability in myself and the other. I regularly fail and my resilience is tested constantly – but I bounce back.

The message of this book is that resilience is not something that you are born with, it is not a mere personality trait. You have resilience and you can develop resilience, we all can. No one can avoid challenges, pain and difficulty in life and at work. We can develop our resilience and our capacity to deal with adversity, loss and change.

Resilience at work

At work we may be asked to work longer hours or to use new technology. We may have to adapt our practice to fit with new legislation, or we may be asked to work internationally. We may face challenging or critical feedback, and be expected to work with difficult people. Our resources may be limited, and we may need to work in a more flexible and speedy way. We may have to manage or face redundancy. In a resilient state, we can deal with these challenges with vigour and enthusiasm. We can remain positive and strong and we can recover quickly from the occasional dip. More likely, though, at some point we may find our confidence eroded by the hurdles and changes we face, and feel sensitive and less robust than usual.

Think of the idiom, *the straw that broke the camel's back*. The camel is a strong creature, capable of surviving in the harsh conditions of the desert, going for long periods without water. Yet even the camel can be broken by carrying just that extra bit of straw. We might all break when we are facing a series of irritations, interruptions, disappointments and disruptions. We are all subject to feeling broken at times, to a breaking down of sorts, of losing our resilience.

Why bounce back?

The title of this book is drawn from the Latin word *resilio*, which means 'to bounce back'; the ability to deal with difficult situations and to recover, to rebound, to get back on track. It is impossible to go through life without challenges, disappointments and traumas from which we will need to recover and get back to work (and life). Resilience is not about forgetting about the difficulties that we have faced, or ignoring the challenge of those adversities; these experiences and difficulties will change us, and they will impact our emotional selves and our response to future crises.

What resilience is about, though, is enabling us to think in times of difficulty, to consider our behavioural and emotional responses despite the challenges we face. In other words, resilience helps us to deal with the situation in a constructive and a creative way. With resilience, we can turn challenges into opportunities, learn from adversity and develop strategies to ensure that the physical and mental collateral is manageable. Picture the weeble doll – no matter how many times the toy is knocked down it bounces back – with a smile on its face. The weeble wobbles, but it doesn't fall down. How remarkable would it be if we could adopt such resilience in dealing with the inevitable knocks we face, both at work and in our personal lives.

This book has been written to help you to bounce back – to give you the resilience to cope with the inevitable failures, knocks and disappointments that accompany all of us – no matter how idyllic life looks from the outside. Resilience can help us not only survive at work, but it can also help us to flourish and develop. It can help us transform difficult and challenging experiences into learning so that our skill and understanding grow. When you face adversity it is understandable that you might feel anguished or angry, yet resilient people seem able to continue to function – physically and psychologically.

Wherever we work and whatever role we deliver, we all have the power to become more resilient, to change our thinking and our response to failure. We will have setbacks, we will be challenged, we will be disappointed, but, drawing on our inner strength, we can bounce back.

Resilience is not binary – you don't have or not have resilience. It is something that can be developed, enhanced and refined. It is my belief that each of us has the capacity to develop our resilience. This book will help you.

How to use this book

This book examines resilience from a number of fresh angles. Each chapter stands alone and can be read and applied on a topic by topic basis. However, if you read from cover to cover you will get the building blocks of the road to resilience – from your internal to your external world, as a follower or as a leader, in times of change or times of loss, times of synergy and team work and times of conflict and disruption.

This introductory chapter sets the scene and introduces the concepts that will be developed and explored in *Bounce Back*. Chapter 1 explores the relationship we have to failure, how this can be crippling for some and prevent us from embracing the learning that comes with trying something that is not certain. Failing fast is not a call to reckless action, but a framework of permission that allows you the space to make a mistake – not mindlessly, not thoughtlessly, but in the process of development and enrichment at work.

Chapter 2 presents the brain and body and their relationship to resilience. Whilst we are talking a lot in this book about emotional resilience, the physical impact of our body and the remarkable capacity of the brain to change itself is fundamental to growing resilience.

Chapter 3 delves beneath the surface. Much of who we are and the way we approach life is formed not just in our recent years but in our early years of life, and even before that, in the womb. This chapter examines the elements of ourselves that are less easy to access, the hidden parts of our identity that shape the way we behave.

In Chapter 4, we examine the inevitability of change and disruption in our working lives. This can cause anxiety, stress and difficulty. We need resilience to cope with change and loss. This chapter examines the way in which we embrace change and offers understanding and tools to cope with inevitable losses at work.

Chapter 5 ventures into the subject of leadership. As a leader or as a follower there are challenges. When we are promoted to a position of leadership, we move from being one of the team to someone different, with different pressures, responsibilities and demands. How can we prepare ourselves to cope with this transition? And how can we as followers deal with the demands of our leaders?

In Chapter 6 we examine conflict, a topic that at times we can have a difficult relationship with. At its core, conflict at work requires us to separate behaviour from the person, the outcome from the intent and the past from the future. Coping with disagreements, perceived attacks and bullying behaviour can disrupt and derail us at work. This chapter examines the topic and offers some constructive tools to help you to develop your resilience in the conflict arena.

Chapter 7 tackles purpose: what is it that energizes you and creates the motivation to work hard? The relationship between our sense of purpose and our resilience is uncovered and the centrality of that bond in coping with adversity examined. The chapter also gives you exercises to reflect on what your sense of purpose is – what drives you to go to work every day? It will be different for us all.

The final chapter ties the key themes of the book together and directs you to further ways in which you can build your resilient self at work. It offers some strategies to examine ideas in more detail; but as we go along, at the end of each chapter there is an exercise, or several exercises, to help build your self-awareness and understanding. These exercises can be carried out multiple times. Some exercises will take you a few minutes, others, such as the *Resilience self-awareness,* may take a longer time as you explore some deep issues worthy of reflection and consideration. Taking the *Resilience self-assessment* test at the start of reading the book and at the end may give you an indication of how your resilience has developed.

The French psychologist Boris Cyrulnik first identified the notion of psychological resilience. His own personal trauma and loss helped him to develop the theory that it is not these experiences that determine our destiny, it is how we respond to that pain and suffering. He wrote about the inner strength we all possess that can set us free, that we are more capable than we imagine ourselves to be. Cyrulnik (2011)[1] drew our attention to the pearl as an emblem of resilience. The pearl is the result of a grain of sand that gets lodged in an oyster shell, the sand irritates the oyster and, to defend itself, it produces a nacreous substance that ultimately becomes something hard, shiny and precious – a pearl.

Wherever you are now in your relationship with resilience, there is potential to develop. You can build your resilience reserves and face your future with excitement and energy. Failure, adversity and change will of course impact on you, but you can bounce back, you can cultivate resilience.

Exercises

Resilience self-assessment

When exploring our resilience, there is often a disparity between our own sense of resilience and the way others see us. It could be that we feel far frailer than we are seen to be... or perhaps because we are quiet, we might be judged as being less resilient. The situations in which we find ourselves can also vary greatly, as, too, can our resilience in these circumstances.

Thinking about yourself at work, how would you rate your sense of resilience? Award yourself a mark out of 10, where 10 is the most resilient. And how would others rate you? Ask a few people (suggestions in the exercise below) to give you a mark out of 10. There is no right or wrong response to the questions posed; the intention of the exercise is to get you to pause and examine yourself a little closer. On a scale of 1 to 10:

- How would you rate yourself?
- How would your partner rate you?
- How would your colleague rate you?
- How would your mentor/coach (if you have one) rate you?
- How would your direct manager rate you?
- How would your friend rate you?

Look at these marks and consider what this might mean. Is there a disparity?

Note: In exploring your self-assessment and the way in which you imagine others see you, it might be worth considering how optimistic or pessimistic you feel you are as a person. Consider how you have behaved when you have had setbacks. Do you find it easy to let go and then carry on, or do these setbacks tend to stay with you?

Resilience self-awareness

Take some time to ask yourself the following questions. Reflect on each topic and this will help you to understand how you assess your relationship to resilience currently. Remember: your relationship to resilience is not static. It can change over time and in different circumstances. This exercise may require some time to complete as you reflect on your experiences. You do not have to rush through each question; take your time and begin to understand your foundations and how the relationship of these key elements of your identity impact your resilience. This exercise will help you to begin to uncover where your potential blind spots might be lurking.

1 Was your family life secure?

2 Did you have to deal with particular trauma or change in early life?

3 Have you had to deal with many challenges in your life?

4 How did you cope with adversities, large or small?

5 Are you a self-confessed pessimist?

6 Or are you an optimist?

7 How quickly do you move on from setbacks and disappointments?

8 How would your colleagues describe the way you deal with setbacks and disappointments?

9 What have you learnt about yourself when you have dealt with disappointment?

10 What support have you drawn on from others?

11 How have you helped yourself to get through difficulties?

Reasons to be resilient

Tick the statement(s) that apply to you.
  I want to be more resilient so that:

1 I can feel more confident.

2 I can be a better manager.

3 I can support my peers.

4 I can get over...

5 I will be less anxious.

6 I will worry less.

7 I will be able to say *no*.

8 I will have a better work–life balance.

9 I can achieve more.

10 I can waste less time on self-doubt.

11 I can enjoy my success.

12 I can apply for promotion.

To further build your self-awareness, rank these in order of importance.
  I want to be more resilient so that:

1

2

3

4

5

6

7

8

9

10

11

12

Resilience scale

Plot yourself on this line of resilience. At one end there is nothing; you are exhausted and without any strength or thought of possibilities for the future. At the other end, you are buoyant, excited, ready to tackle anything. Where do you sit?

Remember: this is not a binary choice and it is not limited by time. You can move along this scale over the course of a piece of work, a project, even a day!

Frail ⟵——————————————————⟶ Super strong

Endnote

1 Cyrulnik, B (2011) *Resilience: How your inner strength can set you free from the past*, Penguin, London

01
Fail fast

Failure is commonly understood as a lack of success; language associated with failure is heavy, and connected to defeat. The demand to succeed first time, every time has been embedded deeply in work culture. Yet failure does not have to be viewed this way – as the end, coming to nothing. Failing might mean frustration, delay or a letdown – but it can also mean that we are discovering our strengths, understanding our market better, knowing who and what to trust. In other words, *learning* from our failures. Indeed, in the world of innovation and startups, without a string of failures you are not taken seriously. To have no failure suggests no imagination, no capacity for expansive thinking, improvement and originality. In this context, the phrase 'fail fast' has become a motif for embracing that spirit of advancement and invention through taking risks, learning from them and moving on quickly to the next challenge or development.

And working life offers so many opportunities for change and advancement: in the world of work, we are entering a Fourth Industrial Revolution. So far, humanity has lived and worked through the introduction of steam power in the 18th century and the power loom that dramatically changed how goods were manufactured. The 19th century brought us electricity and mass production, and from the 1970s on, working life has been revolutionized by computing innovation. Now, we face more developments and transformation with enterprises bringing physical and digital technologies that are changing the way we work and live exponentially. IoT, the Internet of Things, gives us the capacity to transform the way we communicate, exchange and interact. Artificial intelligence, robotic possibilities, digital virtual assistants at work will soon become commonplace. We are communicating in different ways, are accessible 24 hours a day, connect globally and cross-culturally and need to work with pace and agility.

Fear of failure is natural

Each change in the way we work brings with it new challenges and new opportunities, and we can embrace these changes more readily if we allow ourselves the possibility of some failure on the way to our achievements. However, this is often easier said than done. Our reticence to engage with failure is understandable; we live in an age of success and celebration. Much of our popular-media content focuses on entrepreneurial-success stories, and few actually talk about their failures and how organizations and individuals are coping with the consequences of their dreams not being fulfilled.

Failure through the ages

In Greece in 800 BC, merchants whose businesses had failed were forced to sit in the marketplace with baskets over their heads. Unable to see, but seen, they were ridiculed for their errors and endured ritual humiliation for failing to thrive in their chosen commercial endeavour. In premodern Italy, failed business owners with debt were paraded naked amid jeering crowds to the town square. In France in the 17th century, failed business owners were taken to the town centre, where their business collapse was announced publicly. To avoid imprisonment they were forced to wear a green bonnet – a stark symbol of their failure. These examples illustrate how harshly failure has been treated historically.[1]

A fear of failure is completely natural, given the current and historic consequences of humiliation. Today, new entrepreneurs risk scathing newspaper coverage and damning editorial press, not to mention instant online shaming. However, those who fail *and bounce back* – like Richard Branson, Steve Jobs and J K Rowling – do hold a special place in the world's affection. Is this perhaps a hint that the tide is turning? That as a society, we are beginning to recognize that immediate success is not likely for even the most talented of individuals?

The consequences of failure, imagined or real, can stifle innovation and business creation, as can the pain of failure. It is not something that is always easy to recover from. We might need time, good counsel and a degree of grit to get up and have another go. But for any business, institution, creative activity or entrepreneurial endeavour, *failure is always an option*. In some ways it could be said to be inevitable if you are trying hard enough to consider all possibilities. We can't be lucky all the time, things don't always fall into place, people behave unexpectedly, our resources run out, we are depleted. It is important to plan for failure as well as for resounding success.

Failure in different work contexts

This chapter does not go into the reasons for failure. There are just so many potential explanations for business, organizational or workplace ruin: war, recession, taxation, fluctuating interest rates, regulation, poor management decisions. Peter Drucker, the management guru, claimed that the most significant reasons that businesses flounder are a failure to address the key question '*what is our business?*', management continuing with a strategy that is not working or an absence of interest in products or services.[2] But of course, there are also times when organizations face other disastrous events – fires, loss of employees, force majeure. There is also the crushing disappointment of a failed business venture, particularly one that an entrepreneur has felt passionate about and worked on for many years.

And failure is not restricted, of course, to business collapse. We all face disappointments and failure regularly in our working lives: perhaps we are not given the opportunity to present, we are not chosen to go to the convention, we miss the chance to work with the mentor we had so admired. We don't get the opportunity to do what we feel ready, willing and able to do. We do not get the job we had hoped for – seeing a new recruit excitedly take up the job that we had been longing for and had ploughed all our efforts into is extremely tough. The project we are working on does not succeed. Our pitch, of which we are so proud, does not lead to the contract we hoped for. Our newly developed product or service is not chosen by our clients. We don't get a pay rise. Our piece of writing is not selected for a journal.

All industries, professions and organizations benefit from learning from their failures, even when the consequences of that failure are life or death. Failure is not the preserve of those with lesser intelligence or ability; the most accomplished, bright and talented individuals and institutions can experience failure. Denis Waitley, psychologist and self-esteem expert, urges:

> Failure should be our teacher, not our undertaker. Failure is delay, not defeat. It is a temporary detour, not a dead end. Failure is something we can avoid only by saying nothing, doing nothing, and being nothing.[3]

Failure is further described by Waitley as the fertilizer of success; in other words, we need that learning to ensure our future triumphs.

Henry Marsh, author of *Do No Harm,* is a neurosurgeon who has championed the need for failure to be named, even by esteemed and senior surgeons.[4] He cites the essential learning that takes place when mistakes occur in the highly skilled and challenging field of operating on the brain. He says it is important for people in senior positions to speak up, even at the risk of harm to their reputation, as it is only by acknowledging that failures occur in any role that we can be courageous and take risks for the ultimate and better good. If we only worked when there was zero possibility of failure, very little would be enhanced or improved. There would be a danger of stagnation and decay.

Sport offers further evidence of the importance of embracing failure. The basketball player Michael Jordan credits his numerous failures with his stellar success:

> I've missed more than 9,000 shots in my career. I've lost almost 300 games. 26 times, I've been trusted to take the game-winning shot and missed. I've failed over and over and over again in my life. And that is why I succeed.[5]

In the world of academia, talented and bright individuals face regular rejections. For a research grant to be approved, or a paper published, there are gruelling processes of application and review accompanied by a great deal of agony and angst. Professor Dame Jane Francis explains:

> Even now, rejection can make me feel angry and despondent about the wasted effort. And even though it hurts, it's important to think about how you could do it differently next time.[6]

Acknowledging the competitive nature of academic life, or indeed any business venture, can help us recognize the challenges that we face and to accept that rejection is sometimes out of our control; despite our best efforts, we may fail. And we see that sometimes smart and talented people *do* fail, and sometimes they make enormous mistakes. On-demand video streaming services were a relatively new concept in 2000 when Blockbuster executives turned down the chance to buy Netflix for a fraction of its current value. J K Rowling, one of the world's most respected and successful authors, was initially rejected by numerous publishing houses. Karl Lagerfeld dismissed online high-end fashion retail as unworkable, questioning whether anyone would spend considerable money without seeing a garment first. With the benefit of hindsight, we know of the incredible potential and success of Netflix, of Harry Potter and Net-a-Porter.

What, though, can we learn from these mistakes? And how can we turn a loss into a win? Failure may prevent us from applying critical thinking to our next potential business opportunity, by freezing us in the cloud of our mistakes and disappointments. How can we retain a sense of hope following a catastrophic decision or a workplace fiasco? We now go on to examine optimism, hope and resilience in the face of failure.

Optimism, hope and resilience

These capacities have positive connotations and the underlying assumption that both optimism and resilience will have a significant and welcome impact on job performance and work attitude, as a leader and manager, or as a follower. Optimism allows an individual to interpret events as positive rather than negative. This applies not just to performance failures and negative personal happenings, but also to external events and situations. So rather than turning inwards and blaming themselves, such optimistic individuals will explain difficulties in the context of the situation they find themselves in. This model of positive psychology was made famous by Martin Seligman. This oft-quoted psychologist introduced us to the notion of learned helplessness (we'll come back to this later in the book) and the impact of positive psychology on well-being. The by-product of such an attitude of optimism is also the welcome absence of guilt. How might this optimism appear in the workplace? Take the example of the manager who is asked to transfer to another department:

> A manager is transferred to another department unexpectedly. This manager, rather than questioning their ability in their current role, considers external issues – for example, the department was overstaffed, the economy is struggling, they are seen as a flexible individual capable of dealing with change. They interpret the situation positively; they must have needed someone really good and that is why they transferred them. The change is an opportunity, opening up the possibility of further change and growth. This manager has the capacity to bounce back from the assignment they did not seek out

for themselves and use it as an opportunity for further advancement, networking and learning.

One could contrast this with fantasies about being dumped, about being pushed out, about not being wanted. All these feelings create a negative platform from which to experience the transfer. Optimism can give us the best chance to embrace change for the good.

Hope adds another dimension – that of a rekindling of determination and will to succeed even when faced with challenges and obstacles. The hope process allows individuals to see blockages or problems as opportunities to learn, or as a chance for a new challenge. Hope focuses on internal, self-directed agency.

However, hope and optimism are different from resilience. Looking forward with hope and optimism allows us to consider situations, possible causes, threats and opportunities with a positive plan. Resilience is crucial when that positive plan has failed – when there is change and uncertainty and a need for flexibility, adaptability or improvisation. Resilience goes beyond the successes and failures of a particular project or activity; it finds meaning against the odds, in situations that are not easily rationalized or planned for.

Those with resilience recognize that there is a need to both prepare proactively (with hope and optimism) *and* to take certain reactive measures in the face of difficulty and adversity. Resilience in an individual allows them to recognize that setbacks, overwhelming events, positive and negative, can destroy the cheeriest and most optimistic of individuals. People at work need to recover from these challenging events and traumas – they need to bounce back. In these instances, failure can be a springboard for growth.

The resilient know that this is not something that happens at the press of a button. There is recognition and acknowledgement that such an experience will mean that the affected person will need time and energy to recover and rebound, to return to a point at which they can continue to perform. Resilience in this way can be seen as placing a uniquely positive value on situations and risks that might otherwise be viewed highly negatively.

Failure is not just for entrepreneurs

People often speak of failure in relation to entrepreneurial activity. But of course, we can take risks, try new paths and work in different ways without setting up a business. We might simply be driven by a desire for self-improvement, be responding to our employer's demands or reacting to changing client needs or technology. However, when we have invested everything in a new endeavour – financially, physically and emotionally – it can be hard to face that failure, particularly when we are still emotionally connected and still believe in its potential and possibility.

Some of our most successful thinkers, writers and entrepreneurs have taken failure as a chance to be free to try things anew – to persist, refine, redevelop. Think of Thomas Edison, who reportedly declared: 'I have not failed. I've just found 10,000 ways that won't work.' There might be feelings of shame and humiliation. There might be disappointment and financial loss. But there is also a sense of freedom, a chance to start afresh and begin working in a new way.

Slowly, we are beginning to celebrate those who take the risk. Not those who recklessly abandon people and businesses, but those who mindfully recognize that this is the time to stop, consider what has been learnt and walk away with a greater understanding; and that there will be other opportunities to pursue.

If we sailed through our professional, business and personal lives without failure, our experience would be one-dimensional and perhaps even dull. We don't know if something will work until we try it, so we need to develop a mentality where we recognize that we can try to achieve, and if it is not a success and we fail, we can try again… If we fail fast, we can also learn fast.

If we are lucky enough to function in an environment that encourages risks, there is so much to be gained. Not everyone will respond to our failures in an encouraging and supportive way; some will be disappointed and angry. We need to learn to accept the understanding stakeholders and deal with the upset, too, to be clear about our capacity to pick ourselves up and try again. To learn from the failure and to apply that learning for the next venture.

Take the example of the managing director of a leading publishing house thriving in her leadership position, who describes a career risk that didn't pay off. Yet she does not regret her choice, for this is a decision that offered an extraordinary learning opportunity. This bright and ambitious executive took a leadership role in a new sector, as editor of a magazine, and found herself thrust into an alien environment with different timescales, priorities and values. In reflecting on her experience, she describes how six months into the gruelling job, and just when she felt she was getting the hang of it, she was fired – a humiliation but also a relief. This failure taught her about what she really wanted from her working life, the environment she wanted to work in, and the values most important to her. She cites learning about failure as a big part of life: 'You need to stay the course and learn from what does not go well.'

Fail fast, learn fast

So why fail fast?

The notion of a fail-fast system comes to us from systems design. This technology immediately reports an issue that is likely to cause a problem and stop operations rather than continuing with a flawed process. Now business uses the term to encourage bold action to ascertain viability of a long-term strategy or product, preventing years of investment and effort in a methodology that is doomed.

Taking this thinking into our own hands is a further step in helping us as individuals to become more comfortable with uncertainty and to learn to work with situations of failure. When we fail we shouldn't stagnate in that disappointment but review what went wrong, learn from it and think about how that learning can be applied quickly and effectively. It is the mantra that encourages us to get 'back on a horse' after we have fallen off and to learn that next time we should avoid the hurdle that caused us to fall.

Avoiding failure whenever possible seems tempting, as we've seen from the beginning of this chapter. But to avoid failure, you would have to avoid ever doing anything new, and doing the same thing over and over again can mean that you stop producing your best work, as you are not challenged or excited by the work you are doing. You may be doing what you are doing very well – but it may fail to enthuse and motivate you. When you face a challenge, your experience and expertise have led you to a place of competence and capability. Because of this, and the (understandable) fear of failure, you may be reluctant to let that safe place go – maybe you're also surrounded by colleagues and leaders who appreciate your skills and talents and also want you to stay doing what you are doing. However, this can lead to stagnation and eventually to a less-than-sparkling performance, as you are literally dulled. Challenging yourself to do more interesting things brings huge potential but also of course the likelihood that in doing something new you will also not yet be as expert as your previous role – so the sooner you try, the less high-stakes that failure will be. You'll get the dreaded thing out of the way, resulting in some valuable new information... meaning you'll be much less likely to fail again next time.

You got this

When Bobbi Brown left her namesake brand, she felt excitement but also loss and sadness. She was encouraged by a few words of confidence in a chance encounter with a chef who saw her at a party and told her 'Hey you got this.' She went on to adopt this slogan 'I got this!' as a reminder and a motivator to move forward.[7]

VUCA

Innovation brings with it great fluctuation. Predictability and consistency result in safe outcomes but little change or innovation. So pursuing radical change inevitably brings with it failure, error and challenges. Learning to 'unlearn' and to adopt new practice is critical for a breakthrough in technology, innovation or creative development in any field. If we are working in an environment that does not tolerate mistakes of any kind, we are working in an environment that is closing itself off from potential positive change. As Sunnie Giles, author of *The New Science of Radical Innovation* (2018), expresses it, we need to encourage others to fail fast and safely. Then we need to glean lessons learned and disseminate the learning, quickly.

Giles gives us the acronym VUCA[8] to capture the working world of the 21st century – according to her, this period is full of Volatility, Uncertainty, Complexity and Ambiguity. In this climate, failure is inevitable – but it should be welcomed as a means of learning and an opportunity to reset and change direction.

She offers a series of instructions to leaders who hope to innovate radically:

1 Provide an environment where employees can experiment and come up with ideas.

2 Give employees moderate challenges, neither easy nor too hard, in order to encourage creative solutions.

3 Embrace, not just tolerate, failure as essential to radical innovation.

4 Finally, furnish a safe, fast way to fail.

Here's an example of what this can look like in practice. Dame Inga Beale, the first female CEO of Lloyd's of London, describes a tough day she faced when running a Swiss reinsurance company. She writes:

> I had been brought in to turn the company around, but then it was subject to a hostile takeover. I was devastated – it felt as though my child had been taken away from me. I was hysterical for most of the night after hearing the news, but then I got up, put my face on, went to the office and said: 'Right, we're going to fight this.' I let myself be completely absorbed by the shock, then I stood up and carried on, and I didn't shed another tear.[9]

She also identifies the added burden on a leader when struggling with potential catastrophe. The need to cope and bounce back is important for those around you who look closely at your behaviour and take a lead from you. She was able to do this through giving herself time to accept and react to what had happened – not by ignoring it, fearing it, or avoiding the opportunity to fail in the first place by not taking on the difficult job.

Failing fast is not easy

Failing fast is not intended to minimize the demoralizing consequences of a failure. Anyone who has had to tell the people who work for them that a project has failed, or report to their boss or stakeholders that they have not met their goal, will no doubt be at first shattered by disappointment and the consequences of that failure. Only later may the thinking around this being a great learning opportunity surface. It can, at first, be so difficult to deal with.

So whilst of course we shouldn't humiliate those whose businesses have failed, equally, we shouldn't imagine that failing fast is always good, or easy. Embracing failure is essential for anyone in the workplace; as we've seen, it's impossible to avoid it. But we should aim to fail *mindfully* – aware of the impact of the failure, and the responsibility of sharing what we have learnt.

Things are changing, slowly. Some organizations hold 'F... Up Nights'. People are encouraged to share their stories of mistakes and failure, so that the stigma is removed, and the lessons are learnt. There is now even a think-tank called The Failure Institute (www.thefailureinstitute.com); this organization also embraces the notion of 'F... Up Nights'. It was born out of the absence of research into business failure, in contrast to the extensive literature on entrepreneurial success. The Failure Institute aims to encourage study of this subject and the contribution that examining failure can have on future decision-making, policy and business development. The unmentionable is being put on the table and people are being liberated to share their failure stories. None of this means that either startup culture or the celebration of failure is easy; it is challenging, but is part of our world of work and we must learn to embrace it.

Play a Stoic game – what could be worse?

In facing a failure or disappointment we can think like the Stoics. We can consider what else could be worse. Has anyone died? Have we interrupted world peace? Is it the end of world? The central message of this way of thinking is that we don't control and cannot rely on external events; we can only be sure of ourselves and our responses, what we can influence and control.

Stoicism teaches us that the world is unpredictable, that life is short, that we should aim to be strong and in control of ourselves. It encourages us to overcome destructive emotions and to reflect on what can be done and be acted on rather than debated.

One of the tools of the Stoic is to practise misfortune. Montaigne, a 16th-century philosopher, offers us some surprisingly current advice. He urges us to embrace life now, as in death all our options are exhausted. So we should think about all the possible worst-case scenarios that we are afraid of – perhaps redundancy, humili-ation, pay cuts, never being recognized and rewarded – as a way of managing fear and anxiety. Then, when not all these things happen, we can appreciate that most adversity is transient or reversible.

We can also educate ourselves to avoid thinking about good and bad. There is an exercise called 'Turning the Obstacle Upside Down' used by the Stoics that refers to reframing a problem so that every unpleasant, difficult or 'bad' situation becomes a source of good. For example, you are helping a colleague with a task they are struggling with and they respond by being short-tempered, un-grateful and brusque. They are unwilling to cooperate and appear not to want your help. 'Turning the Obstacle Upside Down' would challenge you to think about what new virtues this colleague is directing you to – for example, to patience or greater understanding and empathy.

This is the thinking behind Barack Obama's expression 'teachable moments'. When scandal hit the future president on the election trail, he faced it and turned the negative situation into an opportunity to address difficult issues from a highlighted platform. This is something that entrepreneurs are adept at, taking advantage of opportunities – not in the normal sense of the word – but to turn difficult conditions into a chance to offer new products and services. For example, following the earthquake and tsunami in Japan in 2011, young people and innovators got closely involved in the recovery process, offering innovative and agile reconstruction. Or take the example of Greensburg, the town in Kansas, USA, which, when almost completely destroyed by a tornado, put aside traditional mindsets to rebuild itself as a world leader in environmentally friendly construction. A Stoic turns every obstacle into an opportunity. For a Stoic there is neither good nor bad, only our perception of the situation, and we are in control of our perception.

Self-compassion

We hear about success stories a lot. Of triumph over adversity. Of markets conquered. Of scholarships gained. Seats won. Innovations taken to market. There is an assumption that if you are good, clever and hard-working, you will succeed. But of course, we know that this isn't how working life functions. The good are overlooked, products face production problems, we have a bad day, we make a mistake. Being considerate to ourselves is not excusing the error, but allowing ourselves to consider what went wrong. Were we very tired, or dealing with too much? Did we have family issues that interrupted our thinking? Did we decide to do something because we thought it would please someone else?

It is easy to say 'Get a thicker skin', but it is very hard to accomplish. We are fragile creatures who are largely more vulnerable than we appear, particularly if failure hits us at a time when there are other difficult and distressing aspects to our life. Later in the book we will be exploring loss and change and its relationship to resilience. But there are links here to a failure. It is important to acknowledge that something has been lost, something that your hopes and dreams were invested in has not worked out as you hoped.

Be gentle with yourself

Take the guidance that you would probably give to a cherished friend. It is OK to have a few failures, there is no need to overthink things and be judgemental of yourself. Taking risks will always mean the potential of failure; but without taking risks, nothing will change. Of course failure is not a bundle of laughs; it can hurt to know that something you believed in did not work out. It can be hard to celebrate something that is painful, but the benefit of hindsight can offer you rich learning and clarity. And you are never alone in failure; we are all subject to ongoing failure.

As the chapter has highlighted, no matter our brain power, status, industry, age or gender, failure and rejection will come our way. We will have to cope with disappointment and things that do not go as we hoped. When this happens, we have a choice. Do we descend into despair, and decide never to try anything challenging again? Or do we decide not to brood, to move on and acknowledge that it is a waste of energy to dwell on those things that are outside of our control? We function in a competitive and complicated working world; being gracious and accepting, and learning from our mistakes, failures and disappointments will help us to not live with regret. Failure can be seen as a prerequisite for success... so if you want to succeed faster, double your rate of failure.

Exercises

Permission to fail

We are often hampered by our fear of failure. We don't try new things, embark on new ventures, learn a new skill etc because we demand that we succeed at everything we try and everything we do. What would happen if that demand for success was removed and you gave yourself permission to fail? Take some time to think about what you would do if you knew you couldn't fail. What would you try, what new experience would you encounter?

1 What would you do if you knew you couldn't fail?

2 List the things that you would love to do if success was guaranteed.

3 What is stopping you?

4 What are your fears?

Resilience reserves

We all have reserves that we can draw on in the face of failure, maybe from previous experiences that have taught us that we are able to cope, despite our disappointments and possible humiliation. These reserves are not the same for everyone, but you will have your ways of coping.

What are your resilience reserves?

- Hope – are you able to maintain a hopeful outlook?
- Optimism – do you, despite setbacks, believe in your capability?
- Defence mechanisms – do you protect yourself from failure by denying your involvement? Or perhaps blaming others?

(This isn't a trick question. Defence mechanisms aren't always unhelpful or negative – they can protect us when we need it. Defence mechanisms are dealt with in depth in Chapter 3.)

- Physical well-being – do you take care of your body so that you can maintain energy and strength even at times of great disappointment and failure?

- Mental strength – are you able to process the experience and recognize options for the future, to hold on to your worth and potential?

- Time to recover – are you kind to yourself? Do you allow yourself time to get over setbacks?

- Problem-solving skills – are you able to reflect on the circumstances of your failure and think about how this might have been avoided, or be approached differently next time?

- Social support – do you have people you can turn to, to support you through your time of difficulty?

The confessional

All of us have failed in some way and at some time. There might have been exams that weren't passed, hobbies that have flopped, competitions that were not won. Not to have failed at all in life is a life lived in a very limited way. It suggests that we have stayed in a very safe and limited boundary of behaviour and experience.

1 What is your story of failure (we all have one)?

2 What is it that you have felt ashamed to share?

3 Write down in detail everything that is associated with that failure.

Learning from failure

What are your teachable moments? What have you learnt from your mistakes that has helped you to better manage in the future? Taking time to think about those moments of failure can be difficult for some people. There can be a resistance to dwell on those occasions when things have gone wrong. Yet when we do, we can learn a great deal from that experience. We can learn for ourselves and also for those we work with.

1 Think of a failure you have experienced.

2 What did you learn?

3 What lesson would you share as a result of this failure?

4 How would you respond to the same scenario in the future?

Pre-meditation

It might seem counter-intuitive to practise negative visualization. We are often encouraged to think of the positive, to look at things with a cup-half-full state of mind. However, negative visualization can be something much more helpful than a negative, demoralizing process. Imagining all the things that could go wrong, that could be taken from us, and how foolish we may look helps us to prepare for inevitable setbacks. And it is unlikely that all the negative visualization will come to fruition. This exercise, a useful one to add to your toolkit, was seen by the Stoics as a means of building resilience and strength. Planning and thinking this way prepares you for all eventualities.

1 Think of something that is worrying you.

2 List all the things that could possibly go wrong.

3 What could prevent it from happening?

4 Who might disrupt your plans?

5 What might you do to sabotage the success of this thing or event?

Let go and smile

When we confront a disappointment or failure, we can dwell on that failure incessantly. It can bring us feelings of anxiety and unhappiness. We might replay over and over again the series of events that led to the disappointing ending. We may put our hands to our face in shame. Or avoid people we think know about what went wrong. None of these will help us to learn and move on, though, so instead we need to offer ourselves compassion and let the failure go. Smiling relaxes hundreds of muscles in our face. It also relaxes our nervous system. In smiling, we can offer ourselves that compassion. Try this:

1 Name the failure that you are occupied with.

2 Acknowledge that this was a disappointment that brought you unhappiness.

3 Adopt a position of no blame but increased understanding.

4 Have compassion for yourself.

5 Leave the failure behind.

6 Take the learning with you.

7 Smile.

Learning through our mistakes

When we make a mistake, it can feel disastrous. We can make ourselves suffer and treat ourselves without compassion. Yet the mistake or failure could help us to learn an important lesson, something that will be extremely valuable in the future. When you make a mistake, list everything about this issue that stresses you, point by point, on a piece of paper. Look carefully at your list. Ask yourself: what did you learn from it? What will you do differently next time? Then tear the piece of paper up and dispose of it. You have learnt what you needed to learn, and *that* is what should stay with you – not the feelings of stress from the original mistake.

Endnotes

1 Gasca, L (2018) *Don't Fail Fast, Fail Mindfully*, TED Talk, June, https://www.ted.com/talks/leticia_gasca_don_t_fail_fast_fail_ mindfully (archived at https://perma.cc/526W-6ABG)

2 Cohen, W A (2016) *Peter Drucker on Consulting: How to apply Drucker's principles for business success*, LID Publishing, London

3 Waitley, D (1997) *The Psychology of Motivation*, Nightingale-Conant, Wheeling, IL

4 Marsh, H (2014) *Do No Harm: Stories of life, death and brain surgery*, Weidenfeld & Nicolson, London

5 Kevin Kruse (2013) *Thoughts on the business of life*, https://www. forbes.com/sites/kevinkruse/2013/05/28/inspirational- quotes/#2302c3e76c7a (archived at https://perma.cc/HFK9-ZM6N)

6 What she said: how to handle rejection with grace, *The Sunday Times*, 16 December 2018

7 Stylist Magazine (2018) *Life Lessons from Remarkable Women: Tales of triumph, failure & learning to love yourself*, featuring Bobbi Brown, Penguin Life, London

8 Giles, S (2018) *The New Science of Radical Innovation*, BenBella Books, Dallas, Texas

9 What she said: Dame Inga Beale answers your workplace dilemmas, *The Sunday Times*, 13 May 2018

02
Brain and body

This chapter looks at our internal world, our brains, minds and bodies to understand the role that they play in our ability to bounce back. It also examines our earliest relationships and considers how brain development impacts on our resilience. We look not just at our beginnings, but at the evolution of humankind, and the impact of our survival instincts on the way we deal with stress in our contemporary working lives. This is not a lifestyle, diet or exercise book. Yet in exploring brain function and its relationship to resilience, the body cannot be ignored. How we care for ourselves holistically, including our sleep, will impact our well-being and resilience.

Back to the beginning

Our earliest relationships shape our nervous system, and research has shown that there is a strong link between the development of the brain and our emotional well-being. A good enough foundation in the early years of life is essential to healthy brain development – early interactions between babies and their carers therefore have lasting and significant impact. It can be concerning to think that our emotional style and resources, our emotional resilience, were laid down so early, in the first few years of life. However, recent developments in understanding brain function show that there is so much that can be done to continue to develop and change brain function in later years, indeed at any time in life. We are at an exciting time in terms of flourishing knowledge and understanding about brain development and emotional function. Different disciplines are conversing and converging to help us understand emotional life in a more comprehensive way.

The brain

The brain was at one time thought to be a fixed organ, one that contained a certain number of brain cells and that once those cells were lost or damaged there was nothing that could be done to change it. Thanks to ongoing research, throwing up astonishing and transformative results, we now know that the human brain can indeed change itself; furthermore, that these changes can be effected without medication, operations or physical intervention. That the brain is able to refresh itself and not simply decline is revolutionary – the slow degeneration of the brain was something that was accepted for hundreds of years.

This chapter treads cautiously and recognizes that it is tempting to simplify the complexity of neuroscience research, something that scientists have called 'brain porn'. Claims about assessing leadership, attitude or politics through brain scans is dubious, to say the least. But what I argue is for the potential of the brain to change, adapt and respond.

What relevance does this have for the topic of resilience? What impact can the potential for improved brain function have on our ability to be more resilient, to have greater ability to bounce back from adversity and disappointment? We will discover that the impact is profound. Neuroplastic treatments have helped people recover from strokes, improve memory function, manage obsession, and deal with trauma and sensory deprivation.

Neuroscience allows us to examine the brain and specifically isolate the function of the brain connected to our emotional selves – we are now able to witness the way in which new neural pathways can impact how we function. The technology available to us with data drawn from functional magnetic resonance imaging (fMRI) scans is used as a primary tool of neuroscience. But whilst we can peer into the brain to see how it works, where it is active etc, it can also explain why, or detail the reason for these changes.

Neuroplasticity and the remarkable ability of the brain to change itself have been the subject of extensive research and considerable excitement in recent decades. The terminology 'neuroplasticity' refers to a combination of the nerve cells in our brains and nervous system (neuro) and the quality of changeability, malleability and modifiability (plasticity). The brain can reorganize itself; people can rewire their brain to cope with anxiety, obsession and trauma. What was once thought of as an organ destined for deterioration, and unable to change and adapt, is now recognized as an ever-changing matter, with considerable capacity for transformation and reinvention, laying down new neural pathways that challenge the way we have done things, and opening possibilities for fresh ways of thinking and working.

Rebuilding your emotional brain

The prefrontal cortex is a key part of sophisticated social behaviour; we use this part of the brain to moderate and modulate our behaviour. Early patterns are persistent, as they are part of our early neural pathways and networks – they become emotionally habitual. Yet brain plasticity is considerable, far more flexible and adaptable than originally thought, so that the brain can really change itself.[1] The self-changing brain is a symbol of hope, it embodies the possibility of change – but of course this plasticity might also cause stubborn disorders and unhelpful behaviours too. For the purpose of this book we will focus on the positive impact of plasticity on the possibility to rethink our relationship with resilience.

Pressure and stress

Working under pressure helps the human mind to increase adrenalin production. This in turn allows us to focus, fosters a desire to achieve and a sense of optimum energy and performance.

In this state of pressure, we can 'enjoy our demands'. We can have clear thoughts, be creative and concentrate deeply. Despite being under pressure, we can make decisions quickly and decisively; we are at optimum performance. Yet when we work with stress our concentration is poor, our focus is narrowed rather than expanded. We can feel easily distracted and that our brains are overloaded. In our stress, rather than feeling stimulated and creative, we are more likely to become anxious, to have negative thoughts and to drown in self-doubt with an accompanying absence of self-confidence.

An exciting discovery of neuroscience in the last decade is that the brain is never at rest. Your brain is always engaged even when you feel that you are zoning out. It was referred to in the *Harvard Business Review* as the 'default' network.[2] During this time, the brain is processing existing knowledge. The fascinating element of this discovery is that the brain is capable of an ability outside of our five senses, that of transcendence. In other words, the ability to think about what it might be like to occupy a different mindset, space or perspective. This emphasizes that free time, without allocated tasks or responsibilities, could give us the space for breakthrough innovations. The world of work has picked up on the possibility of this creative space. Google offers its engineers a day a week to work on whatever they want, Twitter holds Hack Week, during which employees leave their day-to-day duties to experiment and play – and other companies have followed suit. In doing so, they have recognized the value of freeing their employees, and their brains, to explore and expand without restriction.

There is undoubtedly much more that could be done to free employees' minds, but in the work environment these initiatives are usually rooted in working structure. However, as an individual, meditation can be a very effective tool for detaching. Having a flash of discovery or a 'eureka' moment when you are not actively involved in work, when you are walking the dog, or cooking supper, can also help to make a breakthrough. And of course, this could also mean the opportunity to develop greater resilience.

Developing a growth mindset[3]

Carol Dweck (2006, 2012) is known for her work on the mindset psychological trait. Her research began in exploring students' attitudes to failure and the difference between those students devastated by small failures and setbacks and those who rebounded. After researching thousands of children, Dweck coined the terms 'fixed mindset' and 'growth mindset' to describe core underlying beliefs about learning and intelligence. If students believed that they could become more intelligent through effort, they therefore *put in* the extra time and effort, and hence enjoyed greater success and achievement. Her belief that developing a growth mindset can help us to make significant changes in our lives is hugely relevant to developing resilience at work.

It is therefore not necessarily about what you currently have, but about what you can develop, what you can gain and what you can find to support you to deal with change and challenges. Hence a growth mindset. A fixed mindset suggests that we have an established repertoire of skills and that this will not change very much once we are adults. A growth mindset is not restricted to the classroom. We can bring this thinking to work. If we believe that we have the possibility of success, that we can think differently and our brains are wired to facilitate that change, that we can cope with difficulties and setbacks, then we will be more likely to do so.

This links to brain plasticity. As we have explored, the brain is more malleable and adaptable than previously thought; connections between neurons can change with experience and practice. New neural networks can be established, and existing pathways strengthened. Neuroscientific research has reinforced the link between recognizing the possibility of changes in the brain, mindset and achievements. Therefore, we can create a growth mindset.

Dweck examines the following areas:

- Skills
  A fixed mindset suggests that you are born with certain skills and that this is unlikely to change. A growth mindset suggests that development is possible, with hard work.

- Challenges
  A fixed mindset relates to challenges cautiously, only engaging with those that are sure to deliver success. A growth mindset sees a challenge as a chance to grow, even if at first you don't succeed.
- Effort
  A fixed mindset looks at effort as a negative quality; if it requires effort and work, then should you be doing it? A growth mindset embraces effort, learning, developing, enhancing your skills as a reward for your efforts.
- Feedback
  A fixed mindset finds feedback very hard; it is received as criticism and felt keenly. In a growth mindset, feedback is helpful, and an opportunity to learn and develop.
- Setbacks
  In a fixed mindset, setbacks are a reason to be discouraged and blame others. In a growth mindset, they are a call for change, a chance to take another path, to work harder or maybe to do something different.

Having a growth mindset means believing that people can change, that they can develop over time. Holding the opposing view suggests a fixed mindset: the assumption that we are who we are and that there is little room for movement or development.

A growth mindset is a prerequisite for allowing behaviour to be challenged – we are not viewing the other as fixed and unchangeable, we recognize the possibility of change and development.

Mental health at work

As thinking, sentient beings we are all susceptible to worries, anxieties and fears. The same intellect that allows us to generate, plan and execute ideas also allows us to fret, worry, catastrophize and imagine that things will go very wrong. At work it is no different; we may be constantly faced with anxiety or issues of worry, but our hope is that we can face these worries and move on – to allow ourselves to turn the page and begin afresh.

We all need to take care of our mental health inside the workplace and outside the workplace. When we are well physically and mentally we are robust, productive and able to engage in life and work fully. Specifically, in the workplace our mental health may be impacted by our environment. This could be in a good way if we are well supported and have a flexible and supportive place in which to work. Or it could be detrimental to our mental health if we are experiencing huge stress, pressure and inadequate support.

Chronic mental illness

As humans, we are generally equipped to function with a degree of anxiety, worry and fear. But some people suffer chronically, for example people with obsessive compulsive disorder (OCD), panic attacks, anxiety disorders, or post-traumatic stress disorder (PTSD). For these sufferers, developing the 'resilience muscle' is almost certainly not the answer. In these cases, medical intervention and therapeutic help are often necessary. This book does not attempt to address these chronic conditions – if you think you might have a mental illness such as these, then you should seek help from your GP or primary healthcare provider.

Work has a vital role to play in our well-being. It can give us purpose and opportunities to grow and expand, so developing our resilience and capability. If, however, we have an existing mental-health condition, it can be triggered by negative work experiences – especially extreme stress, bullying or a toxic environment. We bring our whole selves to work, so if we are suffering with a particular stress at home, be that a loss, relationship breakdown, financial worries or caring for elderly relatives or any other of a multitude of possible worries, those stresses and strains come with us to work.

Everyone is different and can cope with various stresses in different ways. We are also not static and our mental health can fluctuate; in the same way our physical well-being moves on a continuum. It is vital to care for your mental health and to acknowledge that it's as important as your physical health: this is not optional. Finding someone to talk to in your workplace will help you to feel supported and not alone.

Mental health at work: positive-action suggestions

Creating an environment in which people feel comfortable speaking about their mental health is an important way of destigmatizing mental-health challenges. You may be the person who can make changes in your team, or you may wish to raise the following suggestions to help create a more supportive working environment:

- Speak to leaders about making a commitment to mental health in the workplace by offering education in mental health such as Mental Health First Aid Training.

- Think about the space around you. Do you have natural light? Is there somewhere for you to speak to colleagues? Can you see outside? Could you bring a little of the outside in, for example by putting a plant on your desk?

- Can you organize flexible/agile working options for yourself or your team?

- Is there an Employee Assistance Programme or any other way of supporting peers in your workplace?

Enhancing your resilience will help you to cope with workplace stress, but to do this you need to be well. Take care of yourself.

The language of the brain

Are you familiar with some of the terminology we use to talk about the brain and how it functions? Here are a few key words and their broad definitions.

Table 2.1 The language of the brain

Adrenaline	Hormone that prepares the body for fight or flight. You may feel 'adrenaline pumping' before a major presentation or an important event.
Amygdala	The part of the brain that detects threats and is responsible for emotion and survival instincts.
Cortisol	Produced by the adrenal glands, this is known as the stress hormone. High levels of cortisol can negatively impact your mood and well-being.
Dopamine	A neurotransmitter that contributes to well-being.
Hippocampus	Part of the limbic system that controls emotions.
Limbic	The mammalian part of the brain that controls our emotions.
Neocortex	The primate part of the brain where we do our higher thinking.
Oxytocin	Hormone that produces feelings of well-being and stimulates healing and positive interaction.
Parasympathetic nervous system	The part of the body's nervous system that puts a stop to arousal, slowing everything down and relaxing the body. Exhaling activates the parasympathetic nervous system.
Prefrontal cortex	The part of the brain located behind your forehead that is responsible for higher cognitive functions such as decision-making and self-awareness.
Reptilian	The primitive brain that is responsible for survival and aggression.
Serotonin	A neurotransmitter that contributes to well-being.
SSRIs	Selective Serotonin Reuptake Inhibitors can often provide relief from symptoms of distress and depression. These antidepressants can make a huge difference in allowing people to function.
Sympathetic nervous system	The part of the body's nervous system that is responsible for arousal, including the fight-or-flight response. A deep breath activates the sympathetic nervous system.

The body

Taking care of our bodies so that they are able to produce the necessary neurochemicals is essential for our ability to create balance, manage stress and experience well-being. Regular, even gentle, exercise can stimulate endorphins and help provide us with the mental resilience and 'can do' mentality required to face difficulty. Moderate physical activity, such as walking, five days a week, encourages the production of 'happy hormones', in addition to the fitness benefits.

A healthy, balanced diet and good sleep will build our resilience. Watching our caffeine intake, trying to stop smoking, a moderate alcohol intake, and drinking plenty of water will all help.

The power of sleep

If you were offered a product that allowed you to reset your body and your brain to 'healthy', a product that could be utilized every day, was suitable for all members of the population, globally accessible and what's more free, you might imagine worldwide appeal and utter market domination. Well, research suggests that sleep is the most effective way to reset our bodies and brains to healthy, and is something that all of us can access every day, ostensibly for free.[4] Sleep, on the surface of it, is that very wonder drug! There have been thousands of scientific reports that support the value of sleep to human beings.

However, the World Health Organization reports a sleep-loss epidemic in industrialized nations[5] and linked nighttime shift work as a potential carcinogen. If you have ever had to work through the night on a project and then had to continue to work the next day, you will have experienced the impact on your ability to carry out complex tasks, to remember things and acquire new information. An absence of sleep also has an impact on our resilience; we are mentally and emotionally weaker without the sustenance of sleep.

Our decision-making is affected, and so is our emotional stability. When we think of an infant or child crying their heart out we often hear those caring for them explain that 'they are tired'; as adults, we may not yell like a little one, but we are equally impacted. Matthew Walker, a world-renowned neuroscientist, has presented a convincing case for the science of sleep and dreams in *Why We Sleep* (2017). His urgent call is for us each to reclaim our full night's sleep and to do so without shame or embarrassment. Reclaiming this powerful part of our lives will add palpably to our capacity for resilient behaviour.

The comfort zone

When we are learning, we are encouraged to take a step outside our comfort zone, to consider new ideas, to test ourselves in an environment that we have not been in before. Yet as the name suggests, there is much to keep us in our safe place. We might procrastinate to stop ourselves taking that step towards a greater challenge or a task that might not have a guarantee of success. Or we might not speak out at work because we fear we might look silly or reveal ignorance about something that others might be well versed in. We become fearful of that which we don't know, and that fear can even lead to paranoia.

In our evolution, the nervous system evolved to recognize potential danger. There were two options in our development. We could either be wary of potential wild animals hiding in readiness to attack us, even when there was no animal present; or we could believe that there were no dangerous animals, even when there was an imminent danger. We are the ancestors of the first category. We have developed the capacity for needless anxiety, but survival. Those in the second category, who failed to fear the danger of the potential attacking animal, faced death. Our paranoia is therefore adaptive behaviour. We may overestimate the danger of lots of things; but simultaneously, we may underestimate our ability to manage threats.

Our nervous system therefore works in two ways. The parasympathetic nervous system helps us to settle and be calm, to rest and digest. This stops arousal (by which we mean any kind of physical arousal, not just sexual arousal) and essentially slows everything down. It relaxes the body. The sympathetic nervous system, in contrast, is responsible for the fight or flight response. It is accountable for arousal. A good way to differentiate between the way our nervous system works is to think of our breath: when we breathe in deeply, we activate the sympathetic nervous system, when we exhale we activate the parasympathetic nervous system. This is why, when we do calming exercises, such as the 'emotional trigger' exercise, given at the end of this chapter, we breathe out for a longer time than we breathe in – to physically activate this calming and relaxing mechanism.

Emotional triggers

People talk of occasions, individuals, events and even smells that trigger feelings of distress or anxiety. (Note: we're not discussing here the specific and particular phenomenon of triggers in sufferers of PTSD, but more general triggers of negative emotions in everyday life.) For example, it might be that you had a difficult job interview and thereafter imagine every job interview will be as disastrous as that first experience. In this case, without effectively processing the experience, even the mention of the word 'interview' may make you feel worried, insecure or hopeless. Being triggered by negative associations can impact our resilience significantly – not necessarily by the trigger itself, but by how we handle them. If we avoid stressful events, such as never going for another interview, opportunities will be denied to us, and we can create a fantasy of danger and stress that limits our working experience. In this example, the person who is carrying the negative-interview associations will never get a better job or advance in their career, and may well be limited in their day-to-day performance and happiness by simply the discussion of interviews (which is likely in a work environment).

Here's another example. It could be that you see a colleague who appears to be confident, bright and capable in every way – and you compare yourself unfavourably to that individual. Your feelings of inadequacy may be triggered from a sense that you were never as good as your sibling, or that you were humiliated in your early years for not matching up to your caregivers' expectations.

Emotional triggers do not always direct us to self-doubt; they can also cause us to feel angry and aggressive. We may snap because of the tone of a question, or feel enraged or belittled by a small gesture. When you experience this yourself, be aware that expressing your anger or fury will always have consequences. Things that are said cannot be unsaid and there will be costs. Think about what your anger might be concealing: are you hurt? Or does the activity that triggered you make you feel particularly vulnerable? When others express their anger, keep in mind that they, too, may be hiding feelings of vulnerability or hurt.

Take the example of a newly promoted manager who is chairing their first team get-together. They arrive at the meeting feeling anxious and threatened. They are also self-conscious and do not want to appear to be either apprehensive or anything but at ease. The candidate who did not get the manager's job is also at the meeting. In the manager's mind, there is fear of attack, questions of doubt about adequacy and first timer's nerves. This thinking needs to be disrupted. In this example, the manager could repeat reassurances internally: you are basically OK, you did get the job, you were chosen as the right candidate. You may not be perfect, but you will learn, all is well. For the new manager, letting go of their fear and recognizing that there is no need to be so scared will help them to perform better. If you find yourself in a similar situation, understanding that it might trigger feelings of insecurity can be helpful, because it means that you can think it through in advance, and prepare any calming and confidence-boosting tools you might need.

Or perhaps you have been working hard on a project and stayed late to submit some ideas to your manager. Instead of showing appreciation for your efforts they look over your work and point out the faults in what you have done. You are suddenly enraged. This rage is likely linked to your disappointment at your manager's reaction and their failure to recognize your efforts and commitment. If you find yourself in a situation like this, note your reaction, and realize what is at the root of your feelings. This will be far more productive than dwelling on your anger or reacting with aggression. There is an exercise at the end of the chapter to help you.

Somatic intelligence

When our nervous systems are startled, the body responds with a rush of adrenalin that helps prepare our natural defence system – that of fight or flight. If we are constantly bombarded by crises and stress, our capacity to cope is reduced. It is, however, possible to strengthen our somatic intelligence, which is key to our ability to build resilience and cope with adversity. Somatic intelligence essentially means our ability to understand how our body responds to danger, and to use that understanding to help us know how we react in a crisis; in essence, to sooth our nervous systems.

We can recognize when we fall into this startled state: our pupils dilate, and our immune system is repressed. Our hearts race, our muscles tense, we may sweat, become flushed, and our breathing may become faster and shallower. Less obvious might be the decrease in digestion leading to stomach aches or indigestion.

If we experience a threat to our personal safety, a survival response and an acute-stress reaction may be triggered, but the body returns quickly to normal. When we open a door and see someone unexpectedly coming towards us we may jump but we recover quickly. A chronic-stress reaction might be triggered at a lower level; we may not jump in fright, for example, but stress remains active for a longer period of time, and this allows toxins to build up. These chronic reactions might occur when we are working in a very difficult and demanding environment for long periods of time, perhaps with little sleep, little support and whilst taking inadequate care of our physical and mental needs.

There is a helpful notion to prepare us to adapt our physiological state to cope with crisis or challenge. This is known as 'priming' and simply means the way in which we formulate our brain to feel a certain way. This is an activity that we do before an event, to prepare us for what we are about to face, so we may tell ourselves that no matter what, we will remain calm. We might say some positive affirmations before we enter a client meeting for which we are well prepared yet nervous; we might say to ourselves 'I am well prepared,' 'I am the right person to conduct this meeting.' This priming behaviour helps to release oxytocin in our brains and gives us a sense of well-being for whatever we are about to face.

Rational vs emotional creatures

Descartes famously asserted 'I think therefore I am,' suggesting that, above all, humans are rational creatures. Yet there is much to support the notion that our emotional selves drive our decision-making on the basis of our desire and feelings. In fact, we have a dual-system brain. Kahneman and Tversky's Nobel Prize-winning work (2011), entitled *Thinking, Fast and Slow*,[6] illustrated how one system of our brain is fast, emotional and instinctive and the other is slow, calculating and deliberate. The fast element of our brain allows us to respond quickly to situations of immediate danger. As we have shown, these instinctive responses allowed our ancestors to survive. The slow element allows us to think things through carefully and deliberately before acting.

In the contemporary working world we get attached to colleagues, embedded in ways of doing things and strongly connected to people who lead us. Our system of thinking can make us feel instinctively defensive and protective of these relationships. It can also cause us to feel hateful, angry, jealous and revengeful – destructive responses in the workplace. At work the ability to adopt system-two thinking – to slowly think things through and reflect on the consequences of our actions – is so important.

Resilient brains and resilient bodies

This is the bottom line: resilient people do more of the things that care for their brains and bodies. They recognize that the possibility of development and change is there. They do what they can to ensure that they are rested and nourished. When we are feeling less resilient, it is important to develop habits that help us to deal with increased pressure, that allow us to take stock of when our responses are moving from a healthy pressure to a persistent state of stress. Have a look at some of the exercises below – can any of them help you develop better brain and body self-care, for a more resilient you?

Exercises

Building a body of resilience

There are tools available to us to build a stronger and more resilient body. They are also easily accessible to the vast majority of us. Regular exercise, meditation and massage have all been extensively researched and shown to reduce stress hormones, so this exercise is about attending to your physical needs. Can you, for example, take a 15-minute walk during your lunch break? Meditation – is there somewhere you can go for quiet reflection during the day? A park bench? A quiet place to have even 10 minutes of meditative space? Massage – do you have the resource/time and money to allow you to benefit from this method of stress reduction?

Attending to your physical needs

1   Choose one of the following categories:

- exercise;
- diet;
- meditation;
- massage.

2   Write down one change in your chosen category that you will bring to your life.

3   What do you commit to this month?

4   Can you add another category next month?

Examples of building a body of resilience commitments

- Exercise – I commit to walking for 15 minutes a day.
- Diet – I commit to drinking eight glasses of water a day.
- Meditation – I commit to downloading a meditation app and meditating for 10 minutes three times per week.
- Massage – I commit to a massage for myself once a month.

You have the ability to regulate yourself emotionally through taking care of yourself via one of the above methods. But consistency is important: there is no doubt that with any change or shift in behaviour, regular and consistent approaches are most effective. Remember that for new networks to be established in the brain, they have to happen over and over again, until they are consolidated and a new normal is established.

Do you have a growth or a fixed mindset?

Carol Dweck's work on mindset helps us to consider where we struggle to change. Considering each of these categories, review where you sit in relation to skills, challenges, effort, feedback and setbacks.

Table 2.2   Fixed vs growth mindset

Skills

A fixed mindset suggests that you are born with certain skills and that this is unlikely to change. A growth mindset suggests that development is possible, with hard work.

I am...

Challenges

A fixed mindset relates to challenges cautiously, only engaging with challenges that are sure to deliver success. A growth mindset sees a challenge as a chance to grow, even if at first you don't succeed.

I am...

(*continued*)

Table 2.2   (Continued)

Effort

A fixed mindset looks at effort as a negative quality; if it requires effort and work then should you be doing it? A growth mindset embraces effort, learning, developing and enhancing your skills as a reward for your efforts.

I am...

Feedback

A fixed mindset finds feedback very hard; it is received as criticism and felt keenly. In a growth mindset, feedback is helpful and an opportunity to learn and develop.

I am...

Setbacks

In a fixed mindset setbacks are a reason to be discouraged and blame others. In a growth mindset they are a call for change, a chance to take another path, to work harder or maybe to do something different.

I am...

Rescue yourself through sleep

Try and adopt these simple good sleep habits. If you don't get a regular stretch of seven hours of sleep try changing your relationship with sleep in the following ways:

- Avoid stimulants like caffeine and nicotine. They can take up to eight hours to work through our body and can make it difficult to fall asleep.

- Although a nightcap may be inviting, alcohol can rob you of deep sleep. It may relax you, but it will not give you the opportunity for the deepest and most restful of sleep.

- Eating a heavy meal before bedtime can give you indigestion and interrupt your sleep.

- Relax before bedtime; allow yourself time to unwind and prepare for sleep. A hot bath, for example, is known to help you relax and feel sleepy. Or you may prefer to read, or write a review of your day.

- Leave your phone and laptop outside your bedroom. Give yourself permission to be uncontactable and free of distraction.

- Create a sleep schedule. Human beings are creatures of habit, so with sleep, as with any other healthy habit, we should aim for a regular pattern. It sounds counter-intuitive, but try setting an alarm to *go* to bed!

- Note how much better you feel for regular and restful sleep. Make this important.

Calming our nerves

Sometimes our resilience can be tested because of a sense of overwhelming anxiety. It might be triggered by a performance review, or even the anticipation of feedback on a particular part of our performance. We might walk into a conference room and realize that everyone else is holding papers that we have not seen. Or we may feel that everyone is far more senior than us, or indeed that everyone is connected and we are somewhat alone.

For whatever reason – and for each of us it will be something different – we may feel panic and anxiety at work. This exercise is adapted from an approach by Linda Graham (2013), a psychotherapist and meditation teacher.[7]

Calming your anxiety

As far as you can, find a quiet and relatively private space.

1 Place your hand on your heart.

2 Breathe deeply.

3 Exhale longer than you inhale – maybe it will help to count.

4 Hold yourself in a moment of safety.

5 Keep your hand in place on your heart and think of a time when you felt safe, connected and at ease.

6 Stay in this position for 30 seconds.

This simple exercise will release oxytocin: a hormone that makes us feel safe and calm. It is an antidote to cortisol that is released when we are feeling stressed and pressured. If you have not got the space to conduct this exercise you could try simply rubbing the back of your neck; this also releases oxytocin to the brain and can be done subtly to calm feelings of stress.

Endnotes

1 Doidge, N (2007) *The Brain that Changes Itself: Stories of personal triumph from the frontiers of brain science*, Penguin, London

2 Your Brain at Work, *Harvard Business Review*, https:/hbr.org/2013/07/your-brain-at-work

3 Dweck, C (2006) *Mindset: The new psychology of success*, Random House, New York; (2012) *Mindset: How you can fulfill your potential*, Constable & Robinson, London

4 Walker, M (2017) *Why We Sleep*, Penguin, London

5 WHO, *Sleepless in America*, National Geographic, http://www.mysleepapneamd.com/blog/sleepless-america-excellent-national-geographic-documentary-obstructive-sleep-apnea (archived at https://perma.cc/BM66-2QLF)

6 Kahneman, D (2011) *Thinking, Fast and Slow*, Allen Lane, Penguin, London

7 Graham, L (2013) *Bouncing Back: Rewiring your brain for maximum resilience and well-being*, New World Library, Novato, CA

03
Below
the surface

We might like to imagine that what we experience in the workplace is uncluttered, straightforward and above board. However, the human condition is fraught with frailty and imperfection, and these vulnerabilities are (of course) present at work, as well as in our families and in our relationships. There are myriad emotions, motivations, insecurities and drives that are concealed from our colleagues, and sometimes even from ourselves. We're under pressure to perform, often at speed and whilst dealing with new technology and changing personnel. These demands can create a struggle for us as we attempt to moderate our own human condition; for managers and leaders in dealing with their colleagues and those who work with them; and in the development of client relationships.

The aim of this chapter is to heighten your awareness of your unconscious processes, for you to observe daily life at work and your own behaviour, and to consider: what else might be going on? We'll examine some core ideas – based in the work of Sigmund Freud – that will help us to examine work below the surface. We'll consider the unconscious, defence mechanisms and the inner part of ourselves that requires careful investigation and consideration. Greater self-awareness and understanding will help us to be more resilient, to understand where our fears and anxieties are rooted and to find a way to work through these worries.

The unconscious at work – what else is going on?

It's easy to assume that what we see is all that there is to see. That when we observe certain behaviours and actions, they are the sum of the events we witness. For example, we see a manager apparently ignoring a colleague's contribution at a meeting. Or perhaps always looking to one individual for support and expertise. Here, we might be quick to assume that the manager is acting inappropriately, or 'badly', and not setting a good example. While this might be the case, there might also be many reasons for those actions. What we might *not* see or understand are the unconscious motivations causing the manager to act in this way. Perhaps they're envious of their colleague's ideas, or unable to hear the suggestion, as it is out of the ordinary and unexpected. Or perhaps they feel that as the manager they should be coming up with all the 'good' ideas.

When we're on the receiving end of such unconscious projections, it can be hard not to take this personally and blame ourselves. Maybe we assume that we're not asserting ourselves clearly, or not having good enough ideas, or any number of self-degrading assessments. This can cause us stress and make us feel less than worthy. We can question our capability.

Interior and exterior world

It's important to remember, though, that we actually reveal *very little* of ourselves in our interactions, our work and our communication. Most of who we are is hidden below the surface; in the subconscious. These parts of ourselves can, with careful consideration and time, be understood and brought to the surface. Then, buried even more deeply, in the *unconscious*, are the values and inner voices that define our key relationships. Formed in our earliest relationships, these elements of ourselves are (according to the work of Freud) only relieved after intense investigation and by paying close attention to our dreams, our slips of the tongue and perhaps the outcome of an intense psychoanalytic investigation.

The psychodynamic perspective

The *psychodynamic perspective* – the notion that our internal worlds impact our external world and vice versa – is rooted in the work of Sigmund Freud. Though Freud's work moves in and out of fashion, and has been challenged for his patronizing or passé style, his insights were revolutionary and his influence on our culture and world view is pioneering and present. Psychoanalytic theory has been useful in exploring group dynamics, leadership and behavioural norms. It has huge potential to highlight hidden behaviour and offers valuable insights into the world of work.

Freud, of course, is not the only thinker who has encouraged us to get in touch with our inner selves. But the study of the unconscious begins with him, so he's therefore in the spotlight. From this foundation, then, we'll examine the unconscious, and concepts such as psychological defences: ideas drawn from psychoanalysis that provide a useful window into the world of work.

The iceberg model of human consciousness

Figure 3.1   The iceberg model of human consciousness[1]

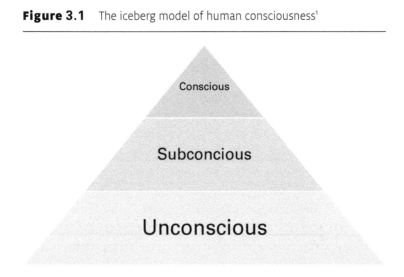

The model in the figure here demonstrates just how little of ourselves is revealed in our day-to-day interactions – if the triangle is one whole personality, only the very tip of the 'iceberg' (the point marked 'conscious') is what we're aware of and consciously revealing each day. This model also highlights that there's a difference between our *subconscious* and the *unconscious*. The subconscious is more easily accessible – with careful examination, we can extract those things that are hovering just below the surface and understand what it is that might be motivating us or causing us to be particularly emotional.

The unconscious, however, is another story. The popular image – of the iceberg with the tip revealing our conscious minds, and the large expansive area beneath the water demonstrating our unconscious – is revealing. There is far more underwater than above, and yet it is the foundation of what we reveal to the world. Much of what is held in our unconscious consists of repressed memories from infancy and childhood. These repressed memories haven't disappeared; they remain part of us. So, if we feel unsafe, envious, neglected or abandoned in early life, these experiences will stay with us long afterwards, buried in our unconscious selves. When the feeling, for example, of rejection or abandonment is triggered later in life, we can attach this experience to our earliest experiences, re-enacting the emotional response buried so deep within us.

Psychoanalysis

Psychoanalysis looks at the unconscious dimensions of *thinking, feeling* and *acting*, and this way of thinking is not just helpful in a clinical setting. Psychoanalytic theory can help us gain greater understanding and insight into our day-to-day lives, including at work. What do I mean by psychoanalysis, and what can it offer us in understanding resilience? Psychoanalysis is both theory and practice. Psychoanalysis as *theory* is the body of work derived from the writings of Sigmund Freud. This work assumes the existence of a *dynamic unconscious*. Psychoanalysis as *practice* refers to the clinical practice of analysis (the person undergoing psychoanalysis) and psychoanalyst (the professional practitioner) meeting on numerous occasions over a sustained period of time. It is also often referred to as 'the talking cure'. There are variations in psychoanalytic practice, but all derive from Freud's work, and rest on the assumption that there are ideas and thoughts hidden from the conscious mind: ideas and thoughts that are brought to the surface through the practice of psychoanalysis.

Why is this relevant? Well, as mentioned previously, psychoanalytic thought and contributions can bring great insight into our understanding both of organizations, and of ourselves *within* those organizations. Working life, as we've said, includes both the conscious and the unconscious self, where – as in every aspect of life – these work alongside each other. The interaction between the conscious and unconscious dynamics at work can be to our advantage, being productive and effective; or these forces can be at loggerheads, creating stress, fear, anxiety and great inefficiency. Exploring our unconscious motivations and patterns of behaviour – understanding whether our conscious and unconscious are working for us or against us, and why – can help us to cope better, and forgive ourselves our frailties. In other words, to be more resilient.

The Id, the Ego and the Superego

According to Freud, there are three elements to our personality: the *Id*, the *Ego* and the *Superego*:

- The **Id** is the first part of our personality to form, and is the source of our drive behaviour. It's primitive and basic, and comprises all the urges and desires that might *not be socially acceptable if we acted on them whenever we wished*.

- The **Ego** emerges later, and has a moderating impact on the Id, reining in drives and forcing us to deal with our desires in a more realistic and socially acceptable manner.

- The **Superego** represents internal rules, our personal guidebook with requirements and values internalized from our parents and our culture. This part of our personality strives to make us behave in a socially acceptable manner.

Our unconscious lives

According to Freud's work, we have *unconscious lives*, and these unconscious lives influence the way in which we conduct ourselves at work. Freud adopted the term *unconscious* in a variety of ways: as a state of an idea or feeling, and also as a system, a place in the mind with repressed contents. There are parts of the unconscious potentially accessible, while other parts are repressed or denied.

At its core, the psychoanalytic view of work is of one influenced by *innate preconceptions*. This term, coined by British psychoanalyst Bion (1959),[2] says that our working relationships, attitudes to groups and to organizational life are influenced by early relationships in family life. So when we lose our job, or fail to get the promotion we hoped for, we feel it not only at the external level, but *also in our internal world*. To understand the way in which our early life experiences impact our current day-to-day relationships, particularly with those in authority, we need to pay some attention to *transference* and *projection*.

Transference

Transference is a very helpful phenomenon. First identified in the therapeutic process, it can be seen in all kinds of encounters and relationships. Transference occurs when our response to an individual and a situation draws on our past experience and encounters. We do this unconsciously, and therefore it's not always easy to identify. Often we're stirred at some level by an individual or experience that reminds us of a past formative encounter – this can occur, for example, when we interact with new situations or people in authority. These environments can take us back to earlier experiences in life, which we then replicate in the transference.

For example, maybe you've found yourself blushing and flustered in a board meeting, something you were well prepared for and competent to participate in... but something in the way the chair spoke to you sparked the experience of the head teacher at your primary school who (in your view) humiliated you. Cognitively speaking, you then expect the *same experience* in the boardroom that you suffered in the classroom. There's good news, though – once you've identified what might be going on, you can be better prepared for the next encounter.

Projection

Projection occurs when we attribute our own thoughts, feelings and responses to another person, so things that cause us to feel, say, uncomfortable, guilty or aggressive might be projected into another person. For example: you may feel hateful towards a colleague (for whatever reason), but you don't feel that it's acceptable to feel hatred – so, you resolve this dilemma by instead deciding that *they* hate *you*.

We can apply this model of attribution to any emotion – including anger and distress. We might accuse another of being angry when we ourselves are fuming, or we might tell someone they're being over-emotional when we ourselves are feeling full of emotion and feeling. Projection allows us to evade an unpleasant insight into ourselves and to deposit it instead into other people.

Psychological defences (defence mechanisms)

As humans, we need to know that we are protected and safe. It's a basic psychological need; this sense of safety is fundamental to our ability to flourish, and is critically established in our early years, formed by how we relate to our parents/caregivers. Feeling that our safety is threatened – whether we feel it consciously or unconsciously, and whether that threat is a physical, emotional or mental one, rational or irrational – causes us to feel anxiety.

We have many ways of dealing with this anxiety; these are called psychological defences or defence mechanisms. They are our ways of coping, and are inherently neither good nor bad. Defence mechanisms help us cope, help us carry on in stressful jobs, meet deadlines and manage our teams – and they can be very useful. They can reduce anxiety; they can provide us with tools to cope.

Figure 3.2   The revealed and protected self

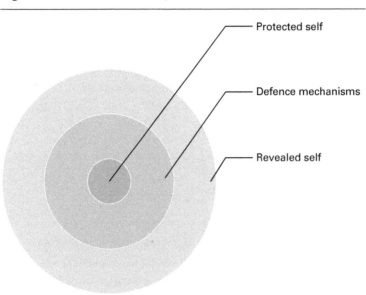

Protected self

Defence mechanisms

Revealed self

It's important to note how we respond to anxiety and to recognize our patterns of behaviour. There's a danger in creating 'blind spots' in the way we conduct ourselves. For example, if I become so used to burying my head in the sand when there's bad news that I am no longer aware of doing it or in control of my reaction, then I could cause damage to the future of my team and place of work. Instead, I need to recognize that I have a tendency to do this – it is one of my defence mechanisms – and this will help ensure that I face up to difficult situations, and find alternative ways of coping when I need to.

An example of a blind spot

Take the case of the deeply committed yet introverted leader. This leader is so keen to listen carefully to everyone's issues and to focus intensely on what is being said that they close their eyes, their way of listening deeply, when you speak. The result is a disconcerting exchange for you, one where the intention was to offer a bounded, prioritized time to really listen – yet you feel left out and confused by this behaviour. Their blind spot, closing their eyes when listening to someone, gets in the way of effective communication. The action intended to elevate the communication exchange actually disturbs it. This action meant the leader literally could not see the impact of his or her well-intentioned yet disruptive style of communication. There is an exercise on finding your blind spots at the end of the chapter.

The Johari window[3]

The Johari window was developed by psychologists Joseph Luft and Harrington Ingham in 1955. They created this model as a method of helping people better understand their relationship with both themselves and others, but it can also be a helpful way of developing your resilience.

If, for example, you see yourself as someone who cannot deal with change, you may avoid situations that stretch you. Yet you might have coped extremely well in scenarios that involved a new approach, showing that you do have the strength and capability to adapt – it might just need others to identify what you are not able to see yourself. We can become stuck in a narrative of identity and overlook the way in which we have changed and developed.

1 In the first square we can locate those things that are known to ourselves and to others, things that are easily accessible. This might relate to technical and practical skills, or known qualities that we are at ease with and are recognized by others.

2 Located in the second square are things that we are not aware of but that are obvious to others; this is the place of our blind spots.

3 The third square is that of our hidden selves; we know but do not wish to reveal this part of ourselves.

4 The fourth square is the part of ourselves deeply buried in our unconscious; neither we nor those around us can see this.

Figure 3.3   The Johari window

	Known to self	Not known to self
Known to others	1	2
Not known to others	3	4

Of course, defence mechanisms don't just function in our working lives; they're evident in our relationships, our families, our communities and in our ability to develop self-awareness.

Throughout our lives, including our working lives, we will be processing pain, confronting our worries and struggling to cope with challenges and anxieties. We all have defense mechanisms that we rely on to cope with the sensitive emotional issues we face in our lives. No matter how much work we do on understanding what our particular approach to dealing with anxiety and stress might be, inevitably we will rely on our defense mechanisms to help us cope and to function. The hope is that, over time and with greater self-awareness, we can become more self-confident and navigate our defense mechanisms more easily.

It's also worth remembering that everyone we encounter, even when they appear to be super confident and at ease, has something that they are struggling with, too. We are not alone.

Danger outside, danger inside

When facing danger from the outside, it can be frightening and challenging. This is experienced in a multitude of ways that can be related to fairly easily – we swerve to avoid a dangerous driver, we duck to avoid a punch, we make sure we're insulated from extreme weather conditions, and so on. However, when the danger we face is coming from *within*, it can't be avoided: it's with us wherever we turn and whatever we do. Personal psychological strength depends on our ability to have a variety of coping mechanisms to allow us to deal with frustrations, failures and disappointments.

Freud's ego defences were developed by his daughter, Anna Freud, in *The Ego and the Mechanisms of Defence* (1937, 1966).[4] Here she elaborated and built on his original ideas, and many other psychoanalysts have added their own ideas about ego defences as a way of understanding our response to suffering and difficulty. We use these psychological strategies to protect ourselves from thoughts and feelings that are unacceptable to us.

The different defence mechanisms that we might employ include:

- repression – burying painful feelings;
- denial – failing to acknowledge emotions;
- rationalization/intellectualization – analyses and thinking rather than feeling;
- sublimation – translating suffering into creative acts;
- turning in on oneself – blaming yourself;

- splitting;
- regression – returning to infancy.

Let's look at how each of these relates to resilience.

Defence mechanisms at work

Repression

A common way of coping with things that feel unbearably difficult is to **repress** these emotions and feelings; to literally push
them into our unconscious so that they no longer interfere with
our day-to-day activities. We can be very skilled at this burying of
hard-to-deal-with emotions! (We can often struggle to let go of
our particular practice of repression – this is why there's often
great resistance to therapeutic input and change.)

Repression places uncomfortable thoughts and feelings in inac-
cessible areas of the mind. When we can't cope, we push things
away – the hope is that we'll forget, or that the emotions will simply go away. The level of 'forgetting' can be anything from a simple
short-term 'parking' of difficult thoughts (for example, putting
aside the emotions after a difficult meeting, to deal with them when
you get home that evening), to a deeply buried anxiety. It's important to understand that the buried memories don't disappear, no
matter how deeply buried, and they can sometimes accumulate and
cause dysfunctional behaviour. According to Freud, our repressed
memories appear in our dreams and in our slips of the tongue
(this is what's meant by the term 'Freudian slip').

For example, maybe you feel extremely disappointed, rejected
and hurt by your failure to be selected for a work project or to gain
promotion. Perhaps these feelings are so difficult to face that you
suppress them – maybe the rejection reminded you of a time when
you were rejected in childhood, or of other painful early memories.
When someone asks you if you're OK with the decision that was
made not to include you in the team, you smile and respond with a
jolly – 'of course not'. As if the issue did not exist.

Denial

One of the most straightforward defence mechanisms is **denial**. Here, we literally refuse to admit the truth of something. This is particularly clear in the case of children: imagine the child with chocolate all over their face who is asked, 'Did you take the chocolate?' '*No, I didn't eat it!*'

In adults, a denial often appears at times of sudden and unexpected loss. Hospital staff regularly see people denying the death of a loved one – 'It can't be true.' In cases of addiction denial is also commonly seen. Alcoholics who deny that they have a problem typically say, 'I can stop whenever I choose.'

This denial can also occur when we fail to face up to disappointment, rejection, stress, bullying and harassment. It can be hard to confront the hurt we feel and so we pretend it isn't there. But the hurt hasn't disappeared. It happened, it's part of us... and so denial provides just a temporary reprieve. Acknowledging the hurt and understanding why we're feeling so rejected will help us to develop a more authentic and long-term response to such challenges.

As a technique to develop resilience, denying our vulnerability can offer a temporary reprieve, but it won't help our long-term ability for sustainable resilience in the face of adversity.

How does all this play out in the workplace? Imagine you've applied for a job that you're very well suited to, and well prepared to take on. You are not offered the post. You accept this, but continue to look for other opportunities. The next job is equally well matched: but once again, you're rejected. You accept this and continue... but when this rejection happens over and over and over again, you might unconsciously process this rejection as too painful and difficult. So instead, you decide that you don't want to change jobs.

In this example, rather than looking at a host of reasons why the applied-for posts might not have been right, you've coped by turning in on yourself and preventing further hurt by repressing, or denying, the desire to move. The desire is 'forgotten' as an escape from the pain of rejection.

Denial is a common defence mechanism. You might see it, for example, in the workplace colleague who is rather short-tempered and irritable, but when asked if there is anything the matter, responds with denial. 'Everything is absolutely fine,' they claim unconvincingly. Or you might have a colleague who's about to make a presentation at a conference and is sweating profusely and high in colour. When you try and say something encouraging to them about their nerves, they deny it entirely. 'I am not nervous, actually I am really looking forward to the presentation. I take these things in my stride.'

In both of these examples, you're left with contrary evidence to what they're saying – but you have also an understanding that you need to play along with this charade, in order to allow your colleagues to function and deliver what they need to. This is the *useful* element of a defence mechanism: it allows us to be protected from our fears and anxieties, to find a way of coping. So if your colleague denies their nerves, or their irritation, somehow they will convince themselves that they can do the presentation or get through the problem, and almost persuade themselves that their nerves will not cripple them or that everything really is fine.

Rationalization/intellectualization

Others cope with the stresses and pressures of work that they find unbearable by **rationalizing** or intellectualizing their difficulties. When faced with a feeling that they're finding hard to cope with, people who rationalize will 'logic' their way out of it. For example, if I miss out on a project that I really wanted to be part of I might say to myself: 'Perhaps I *didn't* want this opportunity *really*. I had far too much to do already, and really, the work would not have been sufficiently stimulating for me to leave my current role. The person I would have been working for was not qualified enough to be a good manager; the team were not skilled in the way I would want them to be.' Any number of reasons might be applied to offer a rationale for why this opportunity was not right for me. In this way, my disappointment and rejection become manageable: 'It was not for me, for very good reason.'

Intellectualization is a similar approach that turns to literature, philosophy or the arts to explain away disappointments and sorrow – so maybe instead of searching for rational reasons, I might channel the works of Aristotle, Foucault or Sartre to *explain* my sadness, and so gain a sense of distance and separation from the feeling – as though observing it from the outside.

Sublimation

Sublimation is often referred to as a mature type of defence mechanism, one in which socially *unacceptable* impulses or idealizations are transformed into socially *acceptable* actions or behaviours; possibly resulting in a long-term conversion of the initial impulse.[5] Sublimation can be a very constructive mechanism for dealing with overwhelming negative emotions. Screaming and shouting at a colleague may release the anger, but will leave a residue of hurt, disruption and animosity, creating an even more toxic environment. Your reputation will be tarnished as someone who can't control their temper, and damage will have been done to your work relationships. However, if you directed that energy into *other activity,* your feelings of frustration and anger might subside. For example, you might reorder the stationery cupboard, or take the opportunity to declutter the office space. *You've sublimated your angry energy into a contextually useful activity.* In this way, sublimation can transform negative impulses into behaviours that do not damage, and might even be productive.

Art and culture is a common arena in which sublimation is at work. Poets, artists and writers might pour their angst into their creative projects, delivering something expressive and generous in which others can benefit from their suffering. The poetry of Sylvia Plath or the art of Picasso or Vincent Van Gogh, or the music of

Beethoven are exemplars of sublimation. Sublimation as a defence mechanism reduces the anxiety that might erupt from unacceptable expressions of urges or harmful stimuli.

Sublimation may also be effective for managing certain personality persuasions. For example, if you have an obsessive need for control of minutiae, you might sublimate that desire into becoming an auditor or librarian, using your potentially disruptive patterns of behaviour for the good.

Turning in on oneself

Another defence mechanism, one that is particularly self-destructive, is the notion of **turning in on oneself**. In this scenario, rather than recognizing that they are being treated unfairly or unreasonably, the individual blames themselves instead. They rationalize the harmful behaviour as something that is deserved and a result of some inadequacy on their behalf. This is a dangerous pattern to get into, as it allows others to treat you in an exploitative way. It's a behaviour pattern that is often seen in abusive relationships, for example.

It can be explained in this way: when it's simply too painful to tolerate the thought that someone crucially important to you is causing you harm – maybe they are cruel, unloving or damaged – instead of facing that difficult reality, you instead decide that the reason you are being treated in this way is because you are unlovable.

In a work context, you might see this translated into a situation where an idealized and respected boss who behaves badly or cruelly is excused, and the employee instead blames themselves. Disappointment in trusted figures can distort a sense of where wrongdoing has taken place. If one tends to project goodness, knowledge and trust onto others with ease, turning in on oneself can be a potential danger zone.

> ### Defence mechanisms in the city
>
> The mechanism of turning in on oneself was evident during the financial crisis in 2008 when, for example, loyal bank employees found it hard to believe that their leaders had betrayed their trust and destroyed their organizations.[6]

Splitting

This defence mechanism – the tendency to polarize – has been particularly evident in the world at large, politics, society and work in the 21st century. Ways of thinking and acting have become more and more divided. It is hard for people to hold more than one opinion and therefore there is splitting into who is right and who is wrong, what is positive and what is negative, who is for and who is against. The likelihood, however, is that the situation is nuanced and complex and this division is unlikely to be helpful. As the International Society for the Psychoanalytic Study of Organisations reports:

> Such polarities accentuate the isolation of individuals and accelerate distance between groups, and can result in rigid and intractable group purpose and association, making coexistence more difficult and impeding our ability to navigate in an increasingly complex, connected and interdependent world.[7]

If we have been placed into an opposing group at work it can feel challenging and isolating. If we are forced into taking sides, and discussion about different possibilities is closed down, tensions can arise at work. Our resilience will be tested.

Regression

Another method of coping with challenges and difficulties is seen in the behaviour of those who **regress**, or become childlike in the face of fear and worry. They claim not to know, that they need help, that they are unable to manage themselves. That they are not really capable. This is sometimes accompanied by a childlike voice and body language more usually associated with a shy child. You might experience them as looking down, hugging themselves, softening their voice and looking at you in a pleading way. They're saying, with words and without: 'Help, I can't cope, please, please rescue me…'.

When we regress, we revert to an earlier stage of development. Rather than handling our unacceptable impulses in a more mature and adaptive way, we are troubled and frightened and behave as children, almost moving back in time. We may fiddle, or giggle, or suck our thumb. Our stress makes us behave as our much younger selves.

Understanding your inner world

The different defence mechanisms are employed to *protect* us from feelings of guilt or anxiety when we feel threatened. Working life is demanding, and it's understandable that we feel threatened or overwhelmed at times. Employing defence mechanisms helps us to cope with the weight of these demands. They're natural and normal – but they can become problematic when they get out of proportion and we use them so frequently that we become neurotic and over-anxious.

Everyone can benefit from exploring and understanding their inner motivations. Knowing who we are, and why we respond to situations in the way we do, can help us not only interact more productively at work but also create greater ease within ourselves. This will, in turn, help us to build our resilience.

Being human brings with it inevitable pain – at work and elsewhere in life. Our defence mechanisms may prevent us from experiencing unbearable feelings, but they may also stop us from facing up to important and necessary realities. Perhaps we are furious about a selfish colleague or abusive leader and we suppress that anger… yet anger can help us to make important changes, to address inequalities and injustices and motivate us to improve the way we live our lives. Perhaps we are too frightened of rejection to recognize the fact that we really want something – a friendship, a promotion, a chance to be part of the senior team. Recurring patterns of behaviour can get in the way of a flourishing career.

Try some of the exercises at the end of this chapter, and think about what you might be doing to protect yourself. To paraphrase the British psychoanalyst Donald Meltzer: 'What lies are you telling yourself to avoid your pain?'

Exercises

Explode or sublimate – self-assessment

At work it is rarely acceptable to lose our control or our tempers. Of course, we're not perfect, and this can happen on occasion, but often we do our best to control that outburst. Think of the last time that you were pushed to your limits and felt an overpowering urge to react. When you're pushed to your limits, what techniques do you employ to manage your emotions? Give yourself a score for each technique, based on the following code:

Key

Reaction	Score
I do this consciously and find it helpful	1
I do this naturally/subconsciously and find it helpful	2
I do not do this, but I think it might be helpful	3
I do not do this and do not think it would help	4
I do this naturally/subconsciously and find it actively unhelpful	5

Thinking about how you react in times of stress can help you manage yourself more constructively in the future. If you know you are likely to see red when you are treated unfairly, then you can think carefully about what to do when this happens. You can count to ten, you can remove yourself from the hostile individual, you can go to the bathroom. Once you're in a position to think clearly, you may be able to choose one of the more constructive ways of dealing with difficulty. But whatever path you take, it is worth considering how you might react in certain situations, as a means of preparing yourself to deal with the adversity in a way that does not damage you, your relationships or your future.

Coping scores

Coping technique	My score
Physical activity	
Go for a walk/run	
Take an exercise class (eg boxing)	
Walk or run home	
Squeeze a stress ball	
Bite your nails or grind your teeth	
Talking cure	
Discuss with a colleague	
Call a family member or partner	
'Vent' with your friends	
Noting techniques	
Write yourself a note expressing your frustration	
Acknowledge to yourself how hard this situation is	
Combat	
Express your frustration immediately, loudly and verbally	
Swear	
Bang the desk, throw something	

Identifying repression – self-reflection

Repression is sometimes called *motivated forgetting*. It is often at the heart of other defensive behaviour, and can be very helpful in relieving ourselves of uncomfortable or unbearable memories. If you see a person behaving in a way that you suspect may be defensive, you could think about the repression that may at the heart of their problem. And for yourself: are you acting in a way that might be hiding your own wounds? Try and reflect on the last encounter you had at work that left you feeling wounded:

- Write down everything about the encounter that made you feel hurt.
- Can you face the painful situation you were reminded of?
- Can you identify what it might be that was triggered by the experience?

The emotionally absent leader – reflection

Having a supportive boss who understands that you have highs and lows at work makes all the difference. As Alexia Inge, the co-founder and co-CEO of online retailer Cult Beauty, writes: 'Employees, like all of us, go through highs and lows. It helps to try to be elastic around people's lives.' This, she suggests, will be rewarded with greater loyalty and flexibility.[8]

Think about a leader you recall who did not do this; one who overlooked emotional needs in order to get a task done (yours or other people's). If you can't think of someone from a work context, use another example – maybe a teacher you had, or a fictional boss from a show or book that you like. Thinking about one interaction in particular, write down your reflections for the following questions:

1 How did you react to this?

2 Were you able to understand their perspective?

3 Were you able to self-regulate, and to recognize the hard work that you had done?

4 Were you able to feed back to the leader how this interaction made you feel?

5 Could you in the future? What might this look like?

Uncovering your blind spots

As the chapter has revealed, we often believe we know ourselves better than we do. We constantly miss things about ourselves and get into a pattern of thinking that does not relate to our reality. We may, for example, decide that we are a terrible public speaker, based on a terrifying and stuttering first experience. Thereafter we define ourselves as incompetent. Yet others view us as accomplished and confident. Or perhaps we are an anxious over-achiever, not really prepared to believe our success?

Take some time to think:

- What is the elephant in your room?
- What is the core story you tell yourself?
- Is it possible that you are hiding a truth from yourself?

Find a trusted colleague and friend and share your core beliefs: do they have a contradictory view of you? Challenge yourself to think of yourself differently. Then, once you have identified some potential blindspots, practise some affirmations:

Instead of: 'I'm a terrible listener.'
Try: 'I'm learning to listen as this is an important skill.'

Instead of: 'I'm a hopeless business leader.'
Try: 'I'm working hard to develop my business acumen and leadership.'

Instead of: 'I'm not popular at work.'
Try: 'I am liked and respected by some colleagues.'

Endnotes

1 Blasko, D G (1999) Only the tip of the iceberg: who understands what about metaphor? *Journal of Pragmatics*, **31** (12), pp 1675–83

2 Bion, W R (1959) Attacks on linking, *International Journal of Psychoanalysis*, 40, pp 308–15

3 Luft, J and Ingham, H (1955) The Johari window: a graphic model of interpersonal awareness, *Proceedings of the western training laboratory in group development*, University of California

4 Freud, A (1937, 1966) *The Ego and the Mechanisms of Defence*, Karnac, London

5 Cherry, K (2018) *Sublimation in Behavioural Psychology*, www.verywellmind.com/4172222 (archived at https://perma.cc/ J2DA-PMT9)

6 Kahn, S (2017) *Death & the City: On mourning, melancholia and loss at work*, Karnac, London

7 International Society for the Psychoanalytic Study of Organisations, www.ispso.org (archived at https://perma.cc/8K77-SSTG)

8 What she said: Alexia Inge of Cult Beauty on dealing with millennial employees, *The Sunday Times*, 11 November 2018

04

Change, disruption and loss

We can be sure of change. There is no individual, organization, sector, industry, culture or nation that will not be impacted at some time or another; things will be disrupted, and things will transform. With that transformation may come some much-needed developments but also, inevitably, some loss. In this chapter we examine the relationship between resilience and change, disruption and loss. We turn positive thinking upside down and confront the inevitable hardships that we will encounter in our working lives, because by facing these head on – the endings, redundancies, disappointments and closures of working life – it can help us to embrace and work with the opportunities available to us. Rather than fear the worst, we imagine the worst and embrace the real.

Change, disruption and loss at work

'Always on' transformation

Globalization, developments in technology, changing work patterns – we are in an era of what has been referred to as 'always on transformation'. Change can be energizing, exciting and transformative. It can take us to new places; establish new relationships; give us a chance to learn a new skill. We can reinvent ourselves, recalibrate our emotional selves, and it can be empowering and thrilling. Just think of all the titles of the self-help books that are out there: *Joy Now!*, *The Power of You...*, *Be Amazing...*, *Create Happiness*. These kinds of personal-development books offer a sense of excitement of what might be and imply a fresher, better, more capable you; an improved you that is just around the corner.

On the other hand, transformation at work can evoke another kind of emotional response. Rather than excitement and anticipation we may feel nerves, anxiety and fear. The sense of 'always on transformation' can be exhausting and draining. We may feel unsettled and challenged as everything we become used to is changed and reshaped. We might wish to hide until the initiative has passed. We may worry about how this change will impact our career plans and whether the new leaders will respect us. We may question whether we will work well with new colleagues or be concerned that we have the right knowledge and skills to work in this new territory.

The gains we gather by change could well mean that we have to give something up. For example, by working more efficiently, we may reduce the number of people working on a project; by improving our technical products, we may limit the opportunity to work things through ourselves. Our digital culture may rob us of the beauty of a handwritten letter, and agile working may offer us more freedom but deny us a tightly knit team.

Even if we are lucky enough to be working in a job that we love, there will be obstacles, changes, challenges and obstructions to test us. What is most relevant is our ability to improvise, to learn to cope with these changes and to build or retain resilience.

Imposed change

When we decide that it is time for a new opportunity, or we want to develop our skills and knowledge through further study, it can be challenging and test us; we will need to be resilient to deal with our chosen path. Yet these represent change that we choose; change that is imposed on us can be particularly hard. We can wait too long to act and end up in crisis, and crisis is exhausting. If we feel loyal to our organization and give our all to our work, then there is an expectation that the organization will be loyal to us – but this is not always the case. So the loss of a job, a change of project, even a shift in teams can feel devastating. Qualities such as loyalty and conformity are often rewarded as strong personal assets to possess in working life, yet flexibility and imagination are often more useful in times of change.

Of course, such attitudes to change are not 'either/or'; we can feel excited and anxious at the same time, and we can respond to change in a range of ways. It could be exciting and thrilling, it could be terrifying and paralyzing. We are living in a time of transition with what might feel like exhausting change – but there are lots of good and bad new ideas and technologies available to us, and we need to be open to these changes and to build our capacity to respond with resilience.

Maslow's hierarchy of needs

In 1943, Abraham Maslow offered a theory of human motivation that is still relevant in our very different world. He proposed that in order to reach the pinnacle of human existence where we achieve our full potential, which he called self-actualization, we need to move through the different levels of emotional development, from physiological needs such as shelter and food, all the way up through love and belonging to self-actualization.

Resilience is relevant at every stage of our development through these levels; and it is important to note that our trajectory is not always *up* the pyramid. We can find ourselves plummeted to the lowest levels in times of despair, when we lose our jobs or our homes, or when we are in dangerous circumstances.

Different responses to change and disruption (can we change for the better?)

Nietzsche famously claimed that 'what does not kill me makes me stronger'.[1] In the midst of hard times, one might not take consolation in this sentiment, of course – yet there is something important here. In facing difficulty, and coping, we can learn that we have inner reserves of strength, that perhaps we are more resilient than we think. When difficulties strike or when disruption enters our working lives, we might respond in several ways:

- move into action mode and do all we can to fix the problem;
- think things through carefully, deciding what this disruption really means, perhaps reorganizing our thoughts and teasing out possible benefits;
- avoid things altogether and deny what is happening;
- console ourselves in destructive behaviour, such as drinking or drug-taking.

In addition, there are some potentially beneficial ways in which we can respond to challenges. Perhaps we might focus our thoughts on the 'why' behind the change. Nietzsche further stated that 'He who knows the reason why can bear most anything.'[2] In this, we can understand the powerful role of sense-making in developing resilience: if we can understand *why* change has taken place, we can 'mentalize' it as the source of our disappointment. This means that we can consider the mental state of ourselves and others, or, in other words – we can process our emotions.

Then, we might bounce back better, stronger, or wiser than we were before. Jonathan Haidt,[3] the social psychologist, explores the benefits of terrible loss, trauma or severe stress. He looks at both the years of research focused on the damaging impact of stress, and the more recent 21st-century examination of the *benefits* of such stress and disruption. In his thinking, we do not simply return to normal functioning after difficult experiences – we go *beyond* that, growing from adversity and fending off damage.

How do you tend to respond to disruptions and challenges? Let's look at some of the ways in which we can respond to change, loss and disruption at work, and then have a go at some of the exercises at the end of this chapter to help you reflect on this.

Responding to change, loss and disruption at work

Some proponents of thinking around resilience focus on the power of positive attitudes. It's a popular and common idea, seen in self-help books, therapies and social media: we can change our circumstances! We will achieve! We will succeed! We will get the job!

A can-do attitude is good, of course. There's a reason why this is such a popular approach, because it works for many people in many circumstances. For example, positive thinking can be helpful in building a strong support network, in caring for yourself, and in pulling positive outcomes out of adversity. However, it's not the *only* approach. An alternative way of exploring resilience is to think about all the possibilities of what might go *wrong*. Bear with me, now! I know this might sound counter-intuitive, but the benefits of looking at the possible negative outcomes, instead of focusing purely on the positive, could well be more helpful in some situations. In Chapter 1, we looked briefly at what we can learn from the Stoics, and it's helpful to consider them again here: we can remember the endless reasons why things are likely to fail, to confront the likelihood that we are probably going to fall short at some time or another, and that circumstances are unlikely to favour us. However, rather than allowing these thoughts to suppress and depress us, we can, like the Stoics, let this be a liberating notion.

Lessons from the Stoics

Stoicism can teach us a great deal about resilience. Stoicism sets out to remind us of the unpredictability of the world and the shortness of life. It is helpful as a reminder of the need to control yourself, to be strong and steadfast. It favours logic over impulse, and doesn't muse about complicated theories of the world but focuses on overcoming destructive emotions. It encourages us to worry only about what we need to worry about, not the 'what ifs' and those things that are outside of our control.

Memento mori – remember death

Reflecting on our mortality may seem an unexpected practice when building our resilience, yet philosophers, beginning with Socrates, entreated us to think about nothing other than dying and being dead. In their minds, this thinking would ensure that we all embrace life to the full and not delay, because life is short and unpredictable – so we should always imagine that life could end right now. If it did, would we be satisfied with the life we have lived? If not… what will we change?

So how might this help us in the workplace? Well, aside from reflecting on your wider relationship with work, work–life balance, and your whole life, we can take these principles and use them in certain contexts. Rather than focusing on death as the inevitable outcome, for example, we can think about the 'death' of our work – in other words, what is the worst possible outcome you can imagine? Is it the loss of employment? The loss of reputation, or money, or clients? If you knew that these things would eventually happen, how would that affect the decisions and choices that you make today?

Respond to what's actually happened, not your fears

Philosopher Epictetus endured slavery to found his own school, where he taught many of Rome's greatest scholars. Born in 341 BCE after Plato's death, he is most associated with refined sensuous enjoyment, often linked to food and wine. Yet his main focus was not pleasure, but the alleviation of misery, much of which he felt was caused by a fear of death. In striving for tranquillity (what we today might call mindfulness), he sought to help people overcome their fear of death.

Facing up to the potential chaos or disastrous outcome of events at work should not cause us to act *too* quickly. Confronting these negative possibilities means that we can think things through and plan for the worst – which is a good outcome and something that can be invaluable in developing resilience. But it can go too far and become unhelpful – at times of change, when rumour and speculation are abundant in the workplace. It's important to remember that there is likely to be far more speculation about the *likelihood* of change and disruption than *actual* change and disruption.

One strategy to cope with all the 'what ifs' is to consider *only the changes that you are presented with*. If thinking through the worst possible outcomes is becoming unhelpful, then change tack – do not stress about possibilities, imagined disruptions or gossip. Prepare yourself for change only when you know it to be a reality. We can then reserve our energies for what is actually going on, to be ready for real rather than imagined change. In this way, the lessons from Stoicism strike a balance – of anticipating the worst and planning for it, and of focusing only on what's actually happened.

Lessons from psychoanalysis

We looked at Freud and psychoanalysis in Chapter 3, and it's relevant again here: meditating on our mortality was a lesson from the Stoics, and also explored in psychoanalytic thought. The unbearable prospect of our mortality can lead many to the delusional thought that they will go on forever. In work terms, this means that people are sometimes unable to see that their time will come to an end in a leadership role or on a project or that the company of which they are part may be subject to collapse and closure.

Markets are fragile, there is global uncertainty and organizations are not immortal. For example, changes in the high street and the development of online retail have created a dramatic change in the way retail markets function. Redundancy, closure, merger and administration are part of our working life. Endings are highly relevant to the world of work in all sectors. There is an absence of lifetime institutions. Our relationship to work is less secure and more transient, and this represents a loss that is worthy of attention and understanding.

Endings provide an opportunity for second thoughts, a chance to reflect on the life that was, the achievements, regrets and the possibilities of that life. Equally, an organization's demise is an opportunity for reflection. There is an exercise at the end of the chapter that gives you the chance to reflect on your life at work, in a day and in a year.

Mourning and Melancholia

Freud explores 'mourning and melancholia' in his 1917 essay of the same name, which tackles the human response to loss. He writes of the process of loss and mourning, and uses an investigation of responses to loss to help us understand what is normal. Freud sets out to clarify the difference between mourning and melancholia.

What Freud referred to as 'melancholia' we would now broadly understand as clinical depression. 'Mourning' is described as a normal reaction to events and one that is carried through with the passage of time. These two approaches to loss are helpful in exploring how resilient we are in the face of loss in our working lives.

During the mourning period, the person realizes that the loved individual or object that is lost is truly gone, and in response, *turns away* from reality. This turning away from reality is marked by dejection, loss of interest and inhibition of all activities. These same symptoms are present in melancholia; however, over time, the mourner returns to their normal state. But the melancholic cannot separate from the lost object and turns inwards.

Recognizing the difference between mourning and melancholia can help us to build greater resilience. This is relevant when we examine our own and also other people's behaviour. When work procedures or circumstances change, some people go through a normal 'mourning period' – they are sad, maybe angry, and struggle to engage fully in their work for a while. However, as they process their emotions, they begin to accept the new state of affairs, and re-engage in their working life. Some, on the other hand, will continue to work as if nothing has changed; there is a deep reluctance to let go of what was a comfortable and well-established way of working.

It is understandable that change is hard at times; it's acceptable to go through a period of adjustment. However, when we are stuck in the ways of the past, unable to recognize what we're doing, or the consequences of this 'stuckness' for others, the difference between mourning and melancholia can be relevant.

Change, limits and mindset

Working with established practice and following existing guidelines certainly have an important place in working life. We need rules and procedures and we need structure and systems. However, over-attachment to 'the way things are done around here' can create a great deal of stress and disruption when change is encountered. Being perfectly organized to deal with the current way of doing things can mean that change is extremely difficult to endure. So when those routines, methods and practices are changed the strength of predictability can become a liability. Where new thinking and innovation are required, an openness to original ideas, creativity and alternative thinking is demanded.

There may be other important factors in making change difficult for some of us. In contrast to the ideas around growth mindset and the work of Carol Dweck explored in Chapter 2, there is an argument that much of the way in which we respond to change runs in our DNA. This does not mean, of course, that there is nothing that can be done to develop our capacity to deal with change and disruption – but it does point to the possibility that change is much more difficult for some individuals than others. And indeed, that some people have a greater emotional resilience than others, too.

Ancient Greeks saw destiny as all-powerful and there is still substance in that notion. Neuroscientist Hannah Critchlow, in *The Science of Fate: Why Your Future is More Predictable Than You Think* (2019),[4] describes how neuroscience is giving us a chance to understand more about how resilience operates, and how we make our own luck through the choices of which environment or relationships we cultivate. She examines what makes one person take one life trajectory and someone else another; what gives resilience and what helps the brain to flourish. Our genetic inheritance and our experience, she argues, lead us to a life that unfolds with less control than we might imagine.

> A growth mindset permeates society... advocating that our every goal or desire can be achieved. We are sold the concept of unlimited agency and capability, a vision of free will on steroids that rejects the idea of constraints, whether biological or socioeconomic.

During our working lives there are moments when we realize that change is required. It could be that we can no longer cope with the international travel of our job, or that we are struggling with our health and need to be closer to our support network, or that we have run out of enthusiasm and passion for something that we once loved. It is often hard, even painful, to change – but we nevertheless choose the change. Even Critchlow, despite her commitment to fate, emphasizes not constraints, but *potential* in building our resilience.

Flexibility, resilience and change

For centuries, work changed very little. We were born into our likely path of occupation and we and generations that followed continued to work in this way. We were farmers, or miners, or factory workers. Where we were born determined the kind of work that we were likely to do for a lifetime. This has changed utterly and completely.

When Adam Smith presented his landmark work in 1776 he showed how the division of labour could make a commercial enterprise much more productive than if each worker took charge of a finished artefact. Workers gave up the satisfaction of producing the whole product and businesses flourished. Workers had to adapt to this change in focus and to a reduction in overall satisfaction and control.

So not only has the kind of work we do shifted from largely physical and manual work and from full production to a division of labour, but technology, culture and communication have created a radical shift in the way we work. We have had to adapt and become flexible. We now need to operate in an 'always on' digital culture, learn to deal with rapid change in virtually every working environment and embrace new skills and challenges on a regular basis.

The relationship between resilience, change and flexibility

As the world of work has changed from inevitable and arduous to uncertain and challenging, we have high expectations of what work can offer us, and we in turn are expected to develop our skills and aptitude at a fast rate. Perhaps we were recruited for a particular project and then asked to work elsewhere, utilizing other skills and knowledge. Or we moved to work with a particular leader who then left the organization. Or new legislation created a need for different practice and procedures. Each change can be a test of resilience. We get comfortable in our position, secure in our knowledge and our relationships – and then we have to work again to establish credibility and trusting relationships.

Remind yourself of the changes you have encountered and survived: technology, location, industry, people etc. Think of the flexibility you have demonstrated in adapting to new working environments, different work patterns and cultures. Recognize the resilience that you have shown in managing these changes. And if your work has been stable and steady and your resilience has not been tested, prepare yourself for the future.

Figure 4.1   The relationship between resilience, change and flexibility

The importance of relationships

As we have identified, adapting well to change is a key feature of resilience. Work is full of such demands to change, be that priorities, policies, products, focus or technology. Change is expected and persistent. Such changes place demands on our resilience reserves, as we know – but an interesting study carried out in 2015 reveals that 75 per cent of the drain on our reserves reported is actually linked to managing difficult people and office politics.[5] Respondents said that managing difficult relationships and politics at work drained their resilience reserves more significantly than being challenged at work or facing upheavals in their personal life. So here, it is the relationships – not the change itself – that prove to be most testing. We will explore the relationship between conflict and resilience further in the next chapter.

A world of agile work

Agile working differs from flexible working. Flexible working relates to the hours that are offered to employees, and includes part-time and other flexible work offerings. Agile work is not about contractual hours and presence, but about output. It offers and values adaptability and freedom, and is in use in major corporations around the world from financial services to tech to government. Agile working offers a way of working based on trust, giving people the chance to do the work when it suits them but also investing in them the confidence that they will be OK on their own to deliver the necessary outputs. Such confidence in people to work without micromanagement or constant intervention is liberating, but it can also require a degree of resilience and self-belief. You are given the tools, information and guidance and then you are trusted to deliver, but you are also left to deliver. You have to create your own system of support.

When we are being led and managed, we might imagine that being left alone is preferable to being given negative attention. Yet research following a survey of over 2,000 Norwegian employees into leadership[6] identifies the negative relational impact of laissez-faire leadership. That when we are 'ignored', this has more negative consequences than if we were treated in an unhelpful way. Being a laissez-faire leader is not just a neutral, zero-leadership experience, but a destructive behaviour causing stress and psychological distress.

This suggests that we do have a need to be seen at work, a need to be noticed and for those who we work for to take account of our contributions. This is reminiscent of Harry Harlow's experiments[7] (1959) and his profound discovery about 'contact comfort', a basic need for young mammals to have physical contact – not just the rudimentary needs at the bottom of the hierarchy of needs. (Interestingly Abraham Maslow was Harlow's first graduate student and the seed of his theory was sown here in his work with Harlow.)

We are not infant monkeys being monitored in a scientific experiment, of course – yet we, too, need to be comforted in some ways at work. We need to have not just our functional needs met, such as instructions and pay; we also need to be soothed to a certain extent, told we are doing well when we are, and steered in the right direction when we go off course. Therefore, when working with independence and autonomy, this should be considered – because without that regular office-based contact, our resilience may be tested.

The velocity of change in the workplace and the future workplace demands that people will be agile and able to embrace and rejoice in change. We will need to adjust to shifting workplaces, expectations, bring new skills, innovate and adapt.

Maintenance

We have seen, then, that change can test our resilience. One of the challenges we face when overcoming adversity is maintaining our ability to function well at work and at home. We can easily be fooled into thinking that we have conquered our difficulties without realizing that there is also a need to invest time in maintaining our resilient behaviour.

You might think of the colleague who has anger issues and is prone to violent outbursts. Following an anger management course, their behaviour improves considerably – but this can only be sustained if the issues from the training are constantly revisited and applied. Without regular maintenance, setbacks will occur. Or perhaps we have recognized that regular exercise will help our wellbeing, and we adopt an enthusiastic programme that peters out after the first few weeks – anyone who has joined a gym in January only to quietly cancel their membership in March will recognize this. When you make a change, it takes work to make that change sustainable.

The same thinking applies to our resilience. We may work hard to develop our strength and capacity to cope with change, yet a small event or disruption can knock us off course. Be kind to yourself when this occurs and remind yourself of your ability to cope. You have done this before and you will be able to do so again – you should aim to 'maintain your gains'.

Our resilience response can also change over time. This is due in part to the challenges that you have to face: for example, being unlucky and having to cope with multiple stressful situations can test anyone's resilience. Dealing with a relationship breakdown might be manageable. But dealing with the breakdown of a relationship, redundancy, harassment and mental-health challenges might be altogether too much. Emmy Werner, whose 32-year longitudinal study in Kauai, Hawaii, followed the lives of 698 children, asks: 'Which side of the equation weighs more, the resilience or the stressors?'[8] In other words – we all have a breaking point.

Catharsis – the writing cure

Catharsis, a word originating in Greek, refers to purification or cleansing of emotions, a purging of feeling that results in renewal and repair. In building our resilience, working through our feelings about change and disruption can be helpful. Naming the fear we have about anticipated changes can help us to understand our deepest worries. Ordering those thoughts in a way that changes our cluttered thoughts into a coherent story can help us to process our emotional response to change, and to see what is really in need of attention. At the end of the chapter there is an exercise to help you with this titled 'Cathartic cure'.

Jamie Pennebaker has written about the value of making sense of adversity through writing in his book *Opening Up*.[9] He examines trauma, and later health and the strong correlation between disclosure and health benefits. His experiment encouraged participants to write about upsetting or traumatic events in great detail. He then followed up their health, alongside a control group who wrote about some other topic. Pennebaker's work supports Freud's notion of catharsis, that in writing or talking about our emotions we are able to process them and to literally 'get it off our chests'.

Bouncing back stronger from change

We are not *either* vulnerable *or* resilient and vice versa. In the same way, we do not *either* embrace *or* reject change. As human beings, we are fluid, and we can learn to engage with change in a way that supports our development and potential for growth.

We really do not know what is coming next and our future work is sure to be full of turmoil and disruption. Yet it may also be a change for the future that we want, a future we can imagine and influence. At times we need courage to do this. As Barack Obama encouraged us, we are the change that we seek. He entreated the American people in his campaign speech that change would not come if we just waited for someone else or some other time: we are the ones we have been waiting for. Or as Brené Brown expresses it, 'When we own our stories, we get to write the ending.'[10] So, we can benefit from adversity, we can create change, we can 'bounce back' not only to where we were before, but to a place of greater strength and understanding.

Exercises

Dealing with unwanted change and disruption

Think about the most recent disruption that you have experienced at work. If you can't call a work example to mind, think about one from your personal life, or a fictional example. Answer the following questions as openly as you can – perhaps you can imagine that you are talking to a very supportive and non-judgemental friend, someone who has your best interests at heart and will listen attentively to all you have to say:

1 Why was this change so difficult?

2 If you were in charge, what would you have done?

3 With the benefit of hindsight, what should have happened?

4 What did you learn from this incident?

5 Did you blame anyone for this event?

6 How would you describe your emotional reaction to this crisis?

7 How do you feel now?

8 Do you often feel like this?

9 Would you prefer to feel differently?

10 Were there any benefits from this change?

Your answers offer you an insight into the way you deal with change. Note your pattern of behaviour: what did you learn about yourself from this exercise? How then will it impact the way you deal with change in the future? If, for example, you noticed that you find developing new relationships difficult, hence working in a new team terrifying, think about ways in which you can build your confidence and skills. Do you have a mentor or a coach at work? Can you explore learning resources yourself? Can you share your concerns with your line manager? Sometimes simply naming the thing that we find challenging can help us, because we can tell ourselves that yes, this is a challenge for me, but I am capable and I will be able to deal with it.

Cathartic cure

Writing down our imagined fears can be a helpful way to process our cluttered thoughts. Take 15 minutes to write down everything associated with an upcoming change in your place of work. Don't worry about the quality of writing, just get everything out – maybe use some or all of these questions as prompts:

- What is going on?
- What do you imagine is going on?
- How will this impact you?
- What is the worst outcome?
- What is the best outcome?
- What are you worried about?
- What are you excited about?
- What skills and talents do you have to cope with this?
- What do you need to learn?
- Who can help you?
- Who can you support?
- What are your strengths?
- What do you want to accomplish?

Working with loss

Loss can be something we work through with sadness and distress, but in a way that allows us, after time, to move forwards. This is what is known as a mourning period. When we find ourselves stuck in loss, unable to see life beyond an ending, we are caught in melancholia. This can be self-destructive and hamper our ability to see a future.

What is a loss you would like to accept?

- Take time to write about what it is that you have lost – this could be a job you loved, a place on a project team, an opportunity, a skill that is lost or a loss from illness or accident.
- What do you miss?
- What are you angry about?
- What could you learn from this loss?
- What did this loss teach you?

Change is coming!"

Imagine you are watching or reading the news, when you see an item about the organization you work for. It begins: MAJOR CHANGES ANNOUNCED AT... How do you respond to this announcement? What is your immediate emotional state:

- excitement;
- happiness;
- anticipation;
- joy;
- fear;
- denial;
- anger;

- worry;
- desire to hide;
- disbelief;
- anxiety;
- curiosity?

Think about what your immediate response may be. This will give you an indication of your relationship with change and your capacity to deal with disruption in the workplace. Of course, this is not always how your mindset will remain – you will learn more, process the information, decide how it impacts on you, your team, your organization and society overall. How might your emotional barometer change over time?

Memento mori

A life in a day

If you were to live your life one day at a time, with the template that 'you may not wake up tomorrow' or when you go to bed, 'you may not sleep again', how would this impact your life and your decisions?

- What would you do today if this was your last day?
- What regrets would you have if this was your last day?
- How can you create a greater sense of urgency in your life?
- What do you really want to achieve?
- What are you capable of that you have denied?
- How would you review your life?

Use those reminders and meditate on them daily – let them be the building blocks of living your life to the fullest and not wasting a second.

A life in a year

Although we can all be certain that we will die, it is nonetheless a fact that we often ignore. The limited time that we have to live our lives, to work in our careers, to flourish in our organizations is often overlooked. Take some time to face this – to acknowledge – 'memento mori' – that one day, you will die. And use this as a spur to think about how you want to live a flourishing life at work. Write down a bucket list – a list of things you would want to achieve. Answer this question: 'What would you do if you only had one year to work?'

Facing our mortality can make us cherish the time and opportunities available to us. It can make us think about what we really want to achieve, what we want to challenge ourselves with and what we consider to be a waste of time. In this way, the inevitable end is a spur to action, to productivity and joy.

Take the CRAB position

The crab is a creature with a thick protective shell. It defends its territory fiercely and can move sideways as well as backwards and forwards. These qualities offer it resilience in the challenging ocean habitat.

Whenever we are confronted with change we have a choice about how we respond to that change. We can retreat, or we can move forwards. Or perhaps we can take a sideways move. We can respond with resilience, we can train ourselves to address change constructively and find other opportunities. The next time you are faced with a change, unwanted or welcomed, take the CRAB position:

C – change or disruption occurs

R – what is your resilient response?

A – what is your attitude to the change or challenge?

B – how are you going to *behave*?

For example:

C – change or disruption occurs

- *The company you are working for goes into administration, your job is at risk.*

R – what is your resilient response?

- *My skills are transferable, I will be able to take my learning with me, I will find another job.*

A – what is your attitude to the change or challenge?

- *I am frightened and disappointed but I will manage this and find another opportunity, maybe it will be even better.*

B – how are you going to behave?

- *I will not blame myself, I will gather as much information as I can, I will spend time seeking advice and exploring opportunities.*

Endnotes

1 Nietzsche, F (1888/1998) *Twilight of the Idols, on Maxims and Arrows*, Oxford World's Classics, Oxford University Press, Oxford

2 Nietszche, F (1888/1998) *Twilight of the Idols, on Maxims and Arrows*, Oxford World's Classics, Oxford University Press, Oxford

3 Haidt, J (2006) *The Happiness Hypothesis: Putting ancient wisdom and philosophy to the test of modern science*, Arrow Books, London

4 Critchlow, H (2019) *The Science of Fate: Why your future is more predictable than you think*, Hodder & Stoughton, London

5 Ovans, A (2015) *Harvard Business Review*, quoting Bond and Shapiro, What resilience means, and why it matters, 5 January

6 Skogstad, A, Einarsen, S, Torsheim, T A, Merethe S and Hetland, H (2007) The destructiveness of laissez-faire leadership behavior, *Journal of Occupational Health Psychology*, **12** (1), pp 80–92

7 Harlow, H F and Zimmerman, R (1959) Affectional responses in the infant monkey, *Science*, **130**, pp 421–32

8 Emmy Werner quoted in *The New Yorker* (2016) *How people learn to become resilient*, 11 February, Maria Konnikova

9 Pennebaker, J (1997) *Opening Up: The healing power of expressing emotions*, Guilford Press, New York

10 Brown, B (2015) *Daring Greatly: How the courage to be vulnerable transforms the way we live, love, parent and lead*, Penguin, London

11 This exercise is adapted from a longer and more detailed class taught at The School of Life, www.theschooloflife.com (archived at https://perma.cc/S6CM-EEMT), where emotional intelligence is taught around the world

05
Leadership

When we have the opportunity to lead, we're keen to do the job well, to be exemplary leaders. We know we have to perform, meet targets and manage resources. But we also need to encourage and motivate, and manage the emotional needs of those working for us. We need to create a climate of trust, be innovative, visionary, challenging and accessible. It's no wonder that leaders can feel enormous pressure to bear the burden of stresses and strains at work – and this requires both strength and resilience. But it can also be hard for those who are 'followers': keen to be supportive and make a positive impression. They may have to cope with less knowledge and power at work, and this too can be challenging. When we are in this position, we need resilience to cope with the times when mistakes are made and decisions are taken without us knowing the full picture. In this chapter, we will explore what resilience means for both leaders and 'followers'.

Leadership and resilience

Resilience in leaders is a two-fold concern: as a leader, you want to be both resilient and support resilience in others.

Being a resilient leader

Leadership is an aspirational and highly examined area of working life. We can go on any number of courses to develop leadership skills and potential; there are thousands of pieces of literature and hundreds of podcasts. In developing our leadership potential, we can strive to become transformational leaders, charismatic leaders, visionary leaders, supportive leaders, authoritative leaders or participative leaders. Leaders are brought in to excite, settle or control. Leadership has so many flavours and interpretations.

Yet to lead, one doesn't need to be in a leadership position. We can inspire, influence, challenge and guide from any stance in the workplace. So, leadership can be a quality that we apply from any position in an organization: we don't need to be the head of a team to be a leader within that team. We can influence and lead through example and character.

In whatever form leadership takes, resilience is often cited as one of the most important qualities that a leader can possess. And this makes sense: in times of constant change, persistent failure and demands for greater returns, resilience is a valuable resource for any leader. The challenges of contemporary working life – restructuring, transition, high staff turnover, product failure and development – can provide the climate in which to develop a resilient leadership posture. In testing and difficult times people look to their leaders to contain and support them, listen to concerns, deal with tough decisions and ensure that their best interests are kept in mind. A great deal is expected of our leaders, so in order to succeed and last, one must be resilient.

Supporting resilience in others

As leaders we therefore have an important role to play in managing the fears and anxieties of those who work for us. Ideally, leaders offer us a bounded space in which to work. This is known as providing 'containment'; literally a safe space to flourish at work, emotionally and physically.

Containment is the process or means of keeping something within limits. In psychodynamic terms, and for our purposes, containment refers to the ability to create a safe space to explore ideas and possibilities; to step outside one's normal realm of operation.

When we have to deal with unexpected difficulties at work – when we lose a contract, or a valued member of staff leaves, or the political or social climate forces dramatic changes on the way we do business – we look to our leaders to contain us, to make it safe to tread in uncharted waters.

Circumstances that test our resilience trigger feelings of insecurity and vulnerability. Not everyone is aware of the impact of added demands on their ability to work effectively, so leaders and managers can provide the containment that allows us to process these events, and help us to see that we are indeed resilient enough to cope.

The relationship between leaders and 'followers'

Leaders and managers have an important relationship with the people who work with them. The leader is often seen as having the knowledge, influence and skills that the person reporting to them does not. These are desirable qualities that make the leader significant. Such dynamics can mean that people could become quite dependent on their leader – particularly if there are stressful situations or demanding times in the workplace. The 'followers' may appear vulnerable and needy, and the leaders may be caught up in providing answers for all worries and concerns. This can prove to be a heavy burden to bear. As we have discussed, leaders need to 'contain' their teams and their people; yet in their drive to be caring and strong, they must be cautious not to sacrifice their sense of self or sap themselves of all their reserves and energy. We'll look at self-compassion a little later in the chapter as a way to pay attention to this balance.

The relationship between a leader and 'follower', then, is not just a cold transaction. In many cases, it can be an emotional rather than a rational relationship at heart. Boundaries are important, allowing the 'follower' to take control of their area of work, and allowing the leader to manage the pressures on themselves. Healthy boundaries encourage people to build their own capabilities, to make some mistakes along the way, with their leader's support and recognition of their achievements. You'll remember the issue of failure, to which we gave considerable attention in Chapter 2. Failure is an essential part of development and growth for those in both leadership and non-leadership positions. As leaders, our job is to listen and respond – not to take everything on board. This is one example of a healthy boundary, and in this way we can help our members of staff to develop their internal capability and resilience without sacrificing our well-being in pursuit of theirs.

How to be a resilient leader

Now let's look at some other ways in which we can, as leaders, implement boundaries and develop our own resilience.

Start small

There are many times when we are confronted with really big challenges and problems. Perhaps a colleague is diagnosed with a terminal illness, or we discover that our company has been sold, or we are embroiled in a scandal that is trending on social media and in the press. These are tough times to build your resilience – don't wait until you are overloaded with issues before you begin exercising your resilience muscle.

We can begin small in learning to cope with adversity. So, for example, you could start by managing your disappointment when your idea is not taken up at a meeting, or when a senior executive forgets that they met you last week. The idea here is that we can actively process our disappointment and hurt, and survive – and *notice* when we do so. This way, we're exercising our resilience muscle, and learning to cope when things do not go as we had hoped.

So, taking leadership one step at a time will help build your confidence and your resilience. You don't have to be the best leader from day one; you can practise and test, and make a few mistakes as you build yourself into the resilient leader you aspire to be. We all know that it is unrealistic to be perfect – except when this applies to ourselves! The exercises at the end of the chapter will help you, whether you are a newly appointed, aspiring, or established leader. Remember: the very best of leaders are always learning.

You are stronger than you know

In our imaginations we are sometimes far frailer than we imagine. We could cope with redundancy; we could deal with working in another environment – even when we feel as though we couldn't. In the main, we are much more resilient than we imagine. See the exercise at the end of the chapter to identify times when you have found the courage and resilience that you did not expect to find.

Self-awareness and blind spots

The Ancient Greek aphorism 'know thyself' is seen as a source of wisdom and knowledge; indeed Socrates is credited with saying that the unexamined life is a life not worth living. In *Leviathan* (1651) Thomas Hobbes used the term 'read thyself'[1] to entreat students of philosophy to look within, stating that there was more to be learnt from examining our own thoughts and feelings that influence our actions than from studying philosophers.

This book, perhaps more gently, encourages leaders to examine themselves, their leadership style and behaviour; to think deeply about the way in which they conduct themselves, how they respond to stress, how they guide and motivate others and how they behave when things do not go well.

We've discussed how, as a leader, you are in a position different from those that you lead. This is both a privilege and a loss. In taking up a position of leadership you lose the ability to speak freely, gossip and share common ground with colleagues. You need to take decisions, decisions that are sometimes resisted, berated and unpopular. Yet as leader, you need to carry out the role in the way that you feel is right – and that sometimes means unpopular actions and choices. No one makes universally appreciated decisions – there is always someone who is less than pleased. This is the lot of the leader. You need to have the resilience to cope with this.

Leaders are often in a state of flux, managing constructive and destructive thoughts, feelings, beliefs and actions that define the way they perform. When we are in a state of anxiety, fear or self-doubt, adversity can hit us hard. We need to learn to quiet the negative voices that interfere with our self-belief and focus, and restore our integrity and inner strength. The first step in doing this is to note that it is happening.

It might be that when something goes wrong you immediately blame yourself, accuse yourself with multiple attacks about what you should have done, what you failed to do, where you have erred. Noting that this is your predilection can be helpful, so that the next time there's a crisis you can pause and think carefully and clearly about what this situation is about. Is this something that you could control? Is it something that you can impact?

Self-compassion

As leaders, we are probably familiar with the idea of being compassionate towards the people we work with. The idea that strong, successful leaders demonstrate compassion, kindness and humanity to those around them is not a new one – and yet, this idea can sometimes fail when we attempt to turn that compassion on ourselves.

But does this matter? After all, self-compassion sounds a bit woolly, or soft. Is it really a robust enough skill to be considered desirable for strong leaders? Well, in short – yes. Psychologists are finding that self-compassion is an important source of coping and resilience.[2]

When we become leaders, especially when that is in a formal leadership role, we move from being one of the team to a different – and sometimes isolated – place. Instead of being able to chat freely with contemporaries, we move into a position of authority. This means we have to be more careful with our speech and recognize that what we say may have implications and a weight and significance, whereas previously what we said might have been taken lightly. Taking on a leadership role also means that we will be subject to judgement, some of which will be favourable and will recognize our talents and strengths. But much of it will be critical, and at times perhaps unfair. In fulfilling our leadership roles, we cannot possibly meet everyone's requirements, and we cannot avoid being the object of blame and hostility when unwanted events occur. As a new leader, you may be finding your way and learning about the way things operate. You may have yet to find your stride or have a clear idea of how you want to conduct yourself as a leader.

All of this adds up to an important conclusion: in order to develop the resilience needed to succeed in this position, we need to offer ourselves a degree of self-compassion, to allow ourselves time to develop our leadership skills. Even as established leaders, it is important to know that we always have scope to develop ourselves and our interactions.

As with any learning, we need to have repeated experiences of the new skill or ability to ensure these changes become part of the way we operate, of who we are. So as leaders we need to establish and reinforce the neural pathways of self-compassion. The idea of 'good enough' was brought to us by the psychoanalyst Donald Winnicott.[3] Winnicott encouraged parents to steer away from aspirations of being 'perfect' parents (for the record, there is no such thing!), and instead to allow themselves to settle for the notion of good enough; to realize that in providing the core needs for their child they were doing enough to ensure their safe and healthy development. This is an idea that is very helpful to apply to leadership. There is no one perfect leader, and we can only strive to do our best, to be good enough.

This is a liberating idea that can allow us to tolerate some mistakes and slack in the way we lead and manage. What's important is that we carry out our role without depleting ourselves of every bit of energy that we possess. This can lead to burnout, and as resilient leaders we want to maintain some reserves of strength for those inevitable setbacks and challenges that will arise.

Manage your critical voice

One thing leaders need to be aware of, and where we may need to practise self-compassion, is our internal critical voice. Changing your inner dialogue, changing the way in which you respond to leadership challenges, is a skill that can be developed. Taking control of your inner dialogue is crucial. Your own resilience is something to value and cherish. Acknowledging that you need to be a resilient leader is a very good first step. Jesse Sostrin, in *The Manager's Dilemma* (2015), describes resilience as a personal act of defiance. He views resilience as an opportunity, a moment to face adversity and reject it, to discard the demand.[4] The exercises at the end of the chapter will help you to identify where you struggle most with adversity.

Figure 5.1   Critical voice

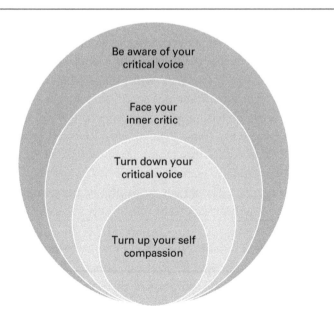

Your critical inner voice may say things like:

- You are the leader; you are supposed to know.
- You're doing a terrible job.
- Someone else would be much more successful.
- I don't think they should have hired me.
- I'm letting my people down.
- I made a big mistake...
- No-one respects me.

In facing your inner critic, you can acknowledge:

- Yes, I am the leader but I am learning.
- There are some things I am doing well.
- It is not helpful to compare myself to others.
- I must have faith that they hired me because I am capable.
- I care about my people; I am doing my best.
- I made a mistake, but I have learnt from it.
- I must learn to respect myself, then respect from others will follow.

Turn down your critical voice:

- Be gentle with yourself.
- This is a new role.
- I have done some things well; list them.
- I bring these skills to the job; list them.
- I wanted the job because....
- No leader is perfect.

Turn up your self-compassion:

- Speak to yourself as you would a valued friend.
- Imagine a team of supportive people around you; what would they say?

- Allow yourself time to learn.
- Seek help where you can.
- Spend as much time thinking about things that you have done well as things that you feel you messed up.
- Note your successes, however small.
- Strengthen your inner compassion by repeating these tasks daily.

Think about your self-compassion and consider how this differs from the way that you treat other people. Deciding to be kinder to yourself will build your leadership capabilities and your resilience.

How are you perceived at work?

We've looked at how we perceive and treat ourselves – but how are you perceived by others at work? Having a clear idea of how we are perceived and experienced by others is harder than it seems. Firstly, we are not mind readers! In order to really know we have to ask people. This can be deeply uncomfortable for some, and even if you find it easy to ask for feedback, it can also be something we worry will not result in an honest reply.

Ask yourself: do you have a clear idea of how you are perceived in your role at work? It is sometimes hard to acknowledge that the persona we think we embody is not the persona that is experienced by others. Is it possible that:

- people see you as critical?
- you are known as someone who is a bit impatient?
- or as not a very good listener?

It may also be that you are seen as:

- a super-accomplished individual who is a bit intimidating?
- someone who rarely makes mistakes?
- someone who makes everything look very easy?

When we work closely with people, it's hard to give them feedback, especially if we have worked with them for some time and patterns are established in the way we work together. Although we might like to feel that we are the sort of person who is very approachable and open to dialogue, we might not be seen in that way. Developing our self-awareness can help us develop relationships by acknowledging where our strengths lie, and how we can foster strong alliances and partnerships. It can also help us see where we need to be cautious, to see the things that we find more difficult – for example, being quick to interrupt, or easily influenced by power or charm. Once we have noted our proclivities, we can then work to manage them. Our self-awareness can help us lead more authentically and build better relationships.

Feedback and resilience – encourage yourself

Much of what we feel about our strengths or weaknesses goes on in our own minds. We build a strong picture of who we are, and what our potential and capabilities are. Most often, we woefully underestimate ourselves, and of course, sometimes we can be inflated about our skills and expertise.

The feedback we give ourselves can be harsh. Developing a kinder approach will allow you to literally cheer yourself on. As the famous saying goes: 'If I am not for myself, then who will be for me? If not now, when?' (attributed to Rabbi Hillel). Psychologist and author Rick Hanson writes about finding inner strength, and urges a focus on guidance rather than criticism.[5] The difference in approaches contrasts the guidance of what's right with the criticism of what's wrong, the potential to build up an individual with the potential to destroy and tear down an individual.

Resilience as a leader and as a 'follower'

As we have seen, leadership brings with it numerous challenges and a need for a great deal of resilience. But there are also demands on 'followers' – those in non-leadership roles. In the past, anyone who wasn't a traditional 'leader' was seen as a 'follower' – someone who is the opposite of a leader. This is a dualism which places the emphasis on the strength of the leader. However, organizations are no longer predictably hierarchical: there are generally flatter structures, networks of teams, and an absence of the dominant command-and-control leadership that used to pervade. 'Followers', or those in non-leadership roles, are essential to the leadership process – without people to lead, there can be no leaders! However, it bears emphasizing that people in non-leadership roles are not necessarily passive, and in times of good team-working and shared responsibility 'followers' have a huge part to play. They, too, require resilience to cope with the demands placed on them. In addition, perhaps most importantly, we should remember that even those in leadership roles often have to interact with – and maybe 'follow' – other leaders. We are all at different times called on to exhibit both leader and follower roles – so it's important to look at resilience in both.

'Followers' are not all the same

Followers come in different forms. There are those that look to the leader to do all their thinking for them, to guide and direct their every action; essentially to micromanage. At the opposite end of the scale, there are followers who are actively engaged and proactive, and who need minimal guidance.

The styles of 'followership' that we explore here were first identified by Riggio *et al*, in *The Art of Followership* (2008). This book identifies five key descriptions of followership styles: the sheep, the yes people, the alienated, the pragmatics and the stars. Do you recognize yourself as a follower or someone in your team in this list? Think about the ways you can respond as a leader to these types of followers in a way that demonstrates your resilience and builds your capacity as a resilient leader:

- **The sheep** – this follower expects the leader to motivate them and do all their thinking. If you are leading a team of sheep, you're constantly worrying about what you will ask of those that work for you, and what they should be doing next. This follower demands much from their leader – they need to be held, directed and supported. Your resilient response will need to acknowledge the fragility of such a follower but gently encourage them to have greater faith in their own offerings, giving them the confidence to support you without constant hand-holding.

- **The yes people** – these are the people on your side, always willing to say yes to whatever you ask of them. Perhaps they rely on the leader to decide what needs to be done, yet whatever you ask of them will be pursued with energy and enthusiasm. These followers are very welcome on any team, but are also a big responsibility for a leader as their blind faith makes them vulnerable to exploitation. This kind of follower can test your resilience, as they project all responsibility onto you: as a leader, you will need to encourage them to express themselves and understand that you do not expect them to only say yes, that you are indeed resilient enough as a leader to cope with some dissent.

- **The alienated** – these are the cynical followers, not willing to follow your lead and full of reasons why the activity is not going to work, but without any viable alternative offered. They can think for themselves, but do so negatively. These followers place demands on the leader; they are the voice of negativity that prevent action moving forwards, so a leader may feel personally attacked and unsupported. These followers can be testing of your resilience. They're not going to display the supportive traits of the sheep or the yes person; instead, they will actively aggravate and challenge. You will need your resilience to ensure that you are focused and clear despite their cynicism, to hold strong in the face of continual critique from this group.

- **The pragmatics** – these usually sit on the fence and work out what is best for them before getting on board. They are attached to the status quo and will only reluctantly let go of existing practice if there is no other option. There is no loyalty here for the leader: this follower is thinking about what is best for them primarily. Such a force within the team can be helpful at planning stages, but when you as a leader have decided on your direction, their input can be unsettling and disruptive. Their personal needs come first, and therefore the leader's thinking about what is best for the team is not going to be a factor for consideration. You will need to be resilient and clear in your decisions and tolerate the reluctance to support you blindly. This is the sort of follower with whom you need to assert your authority.

- **The stars** – these followers also think for themselves, but have a very positive energy. They do not follow blindly, and think things through before accepting a leader's decision. They challenge constructively. Some argue that star followers are leaders in disguise – yet really this is a challenge to the notion that followers can also be independent-minded and demonstrate positive behaviour. This kind of follower will offer a leader a great deal, indeed they can be helpful in coping with some of the less helpful followers listed above. A leader will need to be resilient enough to cope with disagreement and they will need to be able to adapt their decisions to accommodate useful feedback.[6]

The overburdened follower

There will be less empowered followers who might fear appearing weak, or not a team player, taking on more responsibility than they can bear and finding themselves drowning in the demands of work but not wanting to let their leader down. These followers are vulnerable and open to exploitation, consciously or otherwise.

If you are that follower, you need to acknowledge what your tendencies are and try and manage them. If you are managing people who seem to take on everything without question, even when you know they have been overstretched and pushed, you need to be aware and resist the temptation to load the willing subject. As analyst and group-relations expert Wilfred Bion is credited with saying, 'a good leader makes a good follower'.[7] The qualities of listening, understanding and giving support are equally valid for leaders and followers.

Encouraging resilient behaviour

Feedback has been identified as a good way to understand our-selves better and to know how we are experienced by others, but it can also be a way of encouraging resilient behaviour in others. We can help to further build resilience capability by really recognizing when someone has stepped outside of their comfort zone, and ac-knowledging the efforts made to cope with difficulties.

Giving people who work for us the chance to develop and ex-pand their skills can enhance their career prospects and give them an opportunity to test themselves and find out where their strengths and areas for development lie. As a leader, giving your people the confidence to embrace new opportunities sends a strong message of belief in them, which can allow them to have triumphs and suc-cesses that build their self-belief and their resilience.

Particular resilience challenges for leaders

Leaders come in all shapes and sizes, with different personalities, styles, strengths and difficulties. The notion of a leader being just one sort of person, usually of a certain age, a certain gender, and a certain privilege is outdated and unhelpful. Conventional notions of leadership should be challenged; there is more than one way to lead. For example, the idea of the extroverted sales executive is questioned by Adam Grant's work on ambiverts, proposing that those who embody a more flexible way of talking and listening than either the introvert or extrovert (2013) are likely to be more successful.[8]

Introvert or extrovert leader

Carl Jung's perspective on personality brought us the notion of different personality types; different ways of thinking, feeling and behaving. He identified the pattern of introverted and extroverted personality types. Stereotypically, the introvert is at ease with their inner world of thoughts and feelings. The extrovert is more comfortable with the world of people and objects; they are out- ward- rather than inward-looking. These notions are of course binary and do not reflect the complexity of who we are, but they are a useful starting point for self-reflection and self-awareness.

There is an unspoken assumption that a leader is likely to be extrovert, that they will have charisma, magnetism and charm and the potential to woo a room with their networking ability, presen- tation talents and presence. But this notion that only an extrovert can be a successful leader is to be challenged. This leadership bias is designed for the extrovert, the person that thrives in a situation where we brainstorm, working together, sharing thoughts and avoiding quiet contemplation. Introverts can be overlooked. Adam Grant's work (2011) at Wharton points to the finding that intro- verts often create better outcomes, because they allow people to run with their ideas, and allow space for other possibilities.[9] The challenge of the introverted leader, then, is to demonstrate that the best talker is not necessarily the person with the best ideas.

At work, action can be valued over contemplation. Susan Cain's work (2012) on the power of introverts is valuable here, allowing individuals to be at ease with their choices of introversion or extro- version.[10] Connecting to your true self is important. Creativity and leadership are strengths of the introvert, and having the power of solitude to think and develop these ideas is valuable for both the leader and the follower.

Being true to yourself can impact your energy, strength and re- silience. If you need quiet time to energize yourself and tap into your preferred way of working and you are working in an environ- ment where that is not possible, you will suffer. If you are an extrovert who is working as a librarian, expected to be quiet and contemplative, you will suffer, too.

We are all on a spectrum of introversion and extroversion and it is important to note where you sit most comfortably on that spectrum, then you can create the circumstances that allow you to flourish and build your resilience.

Newly appointed leaders

It is challenging to be a leader at any time in your career, but newly appointed managers have a particularly demanding time. There is of course a great deal to celebrate in reaching an important career milestone – but there is also a great deal to learn, manage and communicate. When we are internally promoted, we have a situation where people who were once close peers, even friends, now become people that we manage. It is easy, as a new leader, to fall into the following traps:

- **Micromanaging** – When we become more resilient as leaders, we can let go of the need to control every element of work tasks. We can allow people the space to do their work. Allowing people to feel you trust them is another way to demonstrate your strength as a leader, as is allowing them to make mistakes along the way, as we explored in the chapter on failure.

- **Demonstrating leadership** – As a newly appointed leader you may be keen to establish your authority and show your team the way in which you intend to lead. This can be hard when you are not comfortable with your leadership style and you are still working out the best way for you to take up your leadership position. You might feel particularly self-conscious and you may have to take the stance of 'faking it until you make it'. The model of 'unconscious competence' might be helpful to keep in mind: we all take time to develop flow in our skills and expertise, and leadership is no different.

Figure 5.2   Unconscious competence

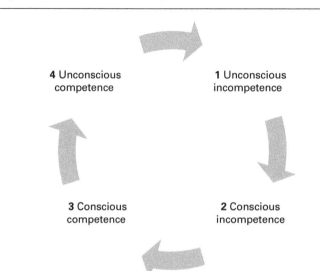

We begin (1) by not even being aware that we are unable to do something – for example, using a new technology. Then, we are made aware and we become conscious of our incompetence and our inability (2). So we spend time and effort and learn the new skill that allows us to work with that technology. This can feel clunky and laboured, yet we can do it: this is conscious competence (3). Finally, after time, we have conquered this new way of working. We do not have to think about it, we can add it to our toolkit and work with flow; this is unconscious competence (4).

- **Not forgiving yourself mistakes** – Any leader will need to give guidance and direction as to what is expected of those that work with them. People may not like the message you convey, or perhaps in the early stages of your leadership career you are not as clear or make some errors (being still in stages 1 or 2 above, perhaps). A common mistake would be to beat yourself up for these mistakes disproportionately; to refuse to forgive yourself for your errors. In contrast, being resilient will help you to overcome and forgive these blips. Remember: when we get something wrong as a leader, we are also demonstrating that we are not perfect. Our intentions are usually well founded and we, too, will learn and develop, as we hope those working for us will.

Developing resilience in yourself and others

Our working lives will offer us many leadership opportunities. These might be conventional and hierarchical, or we might lead our colleagues and co-workers on issues that matter a great deal to us, irrespective of our job title. We may set an example to those more senior than we are, or look up to a newly appointed and junior member of staff. Leadership and followership are interchangeable, and both require a capacity to endure demands and challenges.

As leaders our resilience will be tested. And we will have the added element of working with those we lead to help them to build their resilience and their capacity to bounce back. The exercises that follow will help you to see your existing resilient leadership capacity and offer some ways in which you can develop kindness and compassion for the resilience you need to develop.

Exercises

Recognizing your resilience

There are times when we demonstrate resilience at work, but we don't always credit ourselves with taking a resilient posture. We imagine that if things go wrong we will crumble and collapse. Yet think of a time when something very bad happened at work. Perhaps there was an accident, or you were made redundant, or there was a contract lost that you were sure was yours. There may be other instances that come to mind. Think of how you coped with this adversity:

1 How did you manage?
2 What steps did you take to control your emotions?
3 Who did you turn to for help?
4 What did you learn from this event?
5 How can you apply this thinking to future adversity?

What experience of adversity do you have as a leader?

How have you handled adversity during small challenges and major events?

Small challenges

List three of the small challenges you have overcome. For example, having your idea rejected at a meeting, not being chosen to go to a company event, being overlooked for a promotional event etc.

1

2

3

Big challenges

What major instances have you overcome? Redundancy, loss of a major client, a mistake you made that caused a viral reaction etc. Maybe there is only one – no matter, think about what you have accomplished on this scale.

1

2

3

Self-compassion as a leader

For this exercise, first think of someone to whom you have a duty of care. It could be someone who works for you, and who is in need of your particular care and kindness – perhaps they are returning to work after an illness, or have been deeply disappointed at not being promoted, or perhaps their mental health is fragile or they have some family issues that are taking their toll. Maybe it's not someone who works for you – maybe a friend is going through a tough time, or a family member or child has recently needed your support. Think about the situation, and connect to the feeling of warmth and support that you have for that person.

Now think of *yourself* as someone to whom you have a duty of care and kindness:

- How would you talk to yourself?
- How would you conduct your day?
- How differently would you treat yourself?
- Can you decide to take better care of yourself?

- In making this decision, you can work on strengthening your resolve to care for yourself. Remember: this is not selfish, this is a duty as a leader. You need to use self-compassion to build your resilience – to make you a better leader.

Letter to yourself

Self-compassion can be hard to learn – it can help to think of how you would support someone you cared for deeply. How would you accept their flaws and encourage their development?

List your challenges

What challenges are you facing in your leadership role that are making you feel inadequate? What are the things that you have done, or failed to do, that have made you feel that you are not quite good enough? List the imperfections that are troubling you and causing you angst and worry. Express yourself freely, identifying all your worries and concerns.

Imagine they are someone else's

Take your list of challenges and read it carefully. But do not read it through your own eyes; instead, imagine you are a particularly compassionate and supportive colleague. (Or, you could imagine that the challenges are those of someone you care about and support.) How would this person address your issues? Still imagining you are this person, write a letter to yourself dealing with all your worries. Write with the care, concern and unconditional positive regard that this person would write with.

Come back to it later

Put the letter to one side and take a break. Return to the letter and read your words of understanding, concern and support. This is the feeling of self-compassion. Practise this, often, until it gets easier to treat yourself with kindness.

Self-awareness – what kind of follower are you?

- Do you like to be given precise instructions to follow?
- Are you a loyal and diligent follower?
- Do you need to be persuaded a task is worth doing, or do you follow blindly?
- How do you like to be recognized?
- What kind of relationship do you like with your leader:
  - formal;
  - friendly;
  - lots of direction;
  - lots of freedom?

Once you have a clear idea of your preferred way to follow, instigate a conversation with your manager. Explain your preference and ask them if that works well for them. Be prepared to consider another approach.

Identifying follower types

Earlier in this chapter we identified different follower types, as defined by Riggio. Developing your self-awareness can help you to consider your followership behaviour more carefully and to decide whether you would like to adopt a different approach. As a leader, you may think about the followers you have in your team and the different ways you can support and encourage them.

The type of follower behaviour I adopt is most like:

The sheep – I expect my leader to motivate me and do all the thinking. I will follow instructions but do not think I am capable of more.

The yes person – I am on my leader's side; I will do all I can to support them. It doesn't occur to me to say no to a request, however unreasonable. My leader tells me what to do and I do it.

The alienated – I do not trust my leader; I am constantly questioning whether there are other viable courses of action that would be better. I tend to think negatively.

The pragmatic – I like to make my mind up slowly, working out what the best outcome is for me before I commit. I don't like change for change's sake; it makes me disrupted and unsettled.

The star – I can think for myself. I can challenge decisions, but do so constructively. I am keen to share my ideas and support decisions once they are thought through. I am positive.

The overburdened follower

As a follower, are there times when you worry about appearing weak or not acting as a team player? Have there been occasions when you have said yes to taking on work that you do not have capacity to do? Have you been able to share this with your manager/leader? What steps can you take to relieve yourself? For example:

- Tell your manager you are struggling to cope; try and organize a time for a face-to-face meeting where you can be honest about how you feel.

- Find a trusted colleague and share your concerns.

- Be kind to yourself and accept that you cannot do everything.

- Prepare to say no to some tasks. You cannot do everything.

- Make sure you have time every day to switch off from work.

Endnotes

1 Hobbes, T (1651) *Leviathan*, Penguin, London

2 Neff, K (2003) *Self Compassion: Stop beating yourself up and leave insecurity behind*, Harper Collins, New York

3 Winnicott, D W (1975) *Through Pediatrics to Psychoanalysis: The collected papers of D W Winnicott*, Basic, New York

4 Sostrin, J (2015) *The Manager's Dilemma: Balancing the inverse equation of increasing demands and shrinking resources*, Palgrave Macmillan, London

5 Hanson, R (2018) *Resilient: Find your inner strength*, Penguin, London

6 Riggio, R E, Chaleff, I, Lipman-Blumen, J (2008) *The Art of Followership*, Wiley, Hoboken, NJ

7 Bion, W (1959) Attacks on linking, *International Journal of Psychoanalysis,* **40**, pp 308–15

8 Grant, A (April 8, 2013) Rethinking the extraverted sales ideal: the ambivert advantage, *Psychological Science*, doi:10.1177/0956797612463706

9 Grant, A, Gino, F and Hofmann, D A (2011) Reversing the extraverted leadership advantage: the role of employee proactivity, *Academy of Management Journal*, **54** (3), pp 528–50

10 Cain, S (2012) *Quiet: The power of introverts in a world that can't stop talking*, Penguin, London

06
Conflict

Conflict expresses itself at work in many different ways. It could be two colleagues who don't appear to get along; a tense atmosphere; a heated exchange of words or a formal procedure; or even disciplinary action. Conflict can also be less formal – it can manifest itself in rivalry, or the absence of trust and cooperation. Other behaviour may be even less obvious: people excusing themselves from attending certain events, taking sick leave or requesting to move to another department, or perhaps ultimately choosing to leave the organization. Conflict is not always easy to identify for those not directly involved, yet for parties at the heart of the encounter it's likely to be a significant and consuming tension.

This chapter will look at the relationship between conflict and resilience. We'll consider stress and the way we manage our internal and external conflicts, and look at some strategies and exercises to help us cope with conflict and enhance our conflict resilience.

Understanding conflict at work

Conflict is complex. At its core, it's experienced as a threat, and this leads to feelings of anxiety and fear. And as conflict develops, the consequences of the situation can spiral for the individual, their colleagues and the organization. People take sides, people feel supported or unsupported, those involved in the conflict suffer and those witnessing the conflict are also affected. All of these activities and emotions can test an individual's resilience – so it is important to understand what we mean by conflict; what feeds into conflict at work and the different ways in which it can play out.

The conflict triangle

Conflict is expressed in a number of ways, as illustrated by the conflict triangle below. Thinking about the different parts of a conflict situation, we have the issue itself (problem); the people involved (people); and the events that occur leading up to and as a result of the problem (process). A shift in any one of these elements will create a different outcome and a different degree of disruption.

Conflict is impacted and experienced differently at a **personal** level. This is dependent on:

- the history of relationships – the absence or experience of conflict;
- how experienced you are at conflict at work;
- whether this is the first experience of a dispute at work;
- whether there is a pattern of disputes;
- your state of mind and state of life at the moment (health, family, well-being);
- whether your resilience quotient is low or high.

Figure 6.1   The conflict triangle[1]

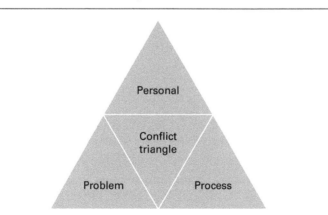

Conflict does not appear in isolation; it is part of a **process**:

- How are people behaving?
- What is the pattern of interaction?
- Who else is impacted?
- How has it spread?
- What has helped?
- What has caused this to escalate?
- What is the culture of the organization?

Then there is the **problem** itself:

- What is the content of the conflict?
- What are the facts surrounding the conflict?
- What are the key issues and interests?
- What are the reasons behind the conflict?
- When did this first emerge?
- How different are the parties' interpretations of the conflict?
- Who is impacted?

There is therefore a great deal to consider when we encounter conflict – and there's huge potential for conflict to spiral, affecting individuals, relationships, tasks and decisions, and sometimes even whole organizations.

Conflict and stress

Conflict and stress are closely linked. In a vicious circle, stress can lead to conflict, and conflict causes stress. In a stressed state of mind, we are vulnerable; we are more susceptible to infection and cold, and small changes impact us greatly. This is particularly so in relationships, where we become less resistant to the words of colleagues, to actions that we perceive as unfair or unkind. Sometimes just being in the presence of someone who stresses us can create imbalance and lead to conflict.

When we have a difficult encounter at work – perhaps our manager calls us into their office and blasts us with criticism that we feel is unfair and aggressive, or a competitive co-worker provokes us – this can trigger an alarm bell in the brain, turning on the fight-or-flight response. Just when we need our wherewithal, our ability to think clearly is shut down. These encounters may last only a few minutes – but it often doesn't end when we leave the office. The ramifications can stay with us and eat into our entire day, even disrupting our evening and our sleep. So the percentage of our working life that is unsettled by the conflict does not necessarily correlate to the amount of headspace that the conflict occupies. We can ruminate and worry for far, far longer.

Don't dwell on it

We will look at some ways to respond to conflict later in the chapter, but one suggestion for dealing with the stress–conflict cycle is this: developing a capacity to 'not dwell' on stressful situations. This might sound easier said than done, but there are tricks and techniques that can help – maybe what works for you will involve creating a distance from the stressful situation by occupying your mind with something that distracts your thoughts. This could be a challenging task, puzzle or even computer game. The worst thing to do after a stressful encounter is to lie back on the sofa and do nothing; that way, the stress will stay with you longer and infiltrate your evening and even day ahead.

Workplace bullying

Bullying, although seemingly related, is a different phenomenon to normal conflict at work. By definition, bullying is conflict that is sustained, repeated regularly over a period of time, and features a one-way power imbalance. Bullying can appear in any organization and any industry. It has been defined as follows:

> Bullying at work means harassing, offending, socially excluding someone or negatively affecting someone's work tasks. . . it has to occur repeatedly and regularly (eg weekly) and over a period of time (eg about six months). Bullying is an escalating process in the course of which the person confronted ends up in an inferior position and becomes the target of systematic negative social acts. A conflict cannot be called bullying if the incident is an isolated event or if two parties of approximately equal 'strength' are in conflict.[2]

Bullying has a negative impact on the well-being of its targets, psychologically and physically, but it also impacts those who are bystanders to the offences and those accused of bullying. It causes feelings of distress, humiliation and offence, and disrupts work, as well as creating an unpleasant working environment for all those experiencing and witnessing the behaviour.

All bullying situations are different; they can be complex and individuals can respond in different ways. We may have a diverse tolerance and threshold for bullying behaviour in different contexts and at different times. If it is the first time that you have faced a bullying scenario, you will be differently equipped than if you have been through this experience before. Whether it is the first time or a second or third bullying situation, if you are facing a workplace bullying situation there are steps you can take to protect yourself.

Aryanne Oade explores the pitfalls of workplace bullying and presents some strategies to *Become Bully-Proof and Regain Control of Your Life* (2015). She suggests:

- Try and respond in a timely way, ie quickly. This will mean that the issues can be addressed without escalating.

- Put the issues back to the bully, speak clearly and explain what the facts are. Most bullying language contains only elements of truth.

- Try and adopt confident body language. The bully is playing with power. Show them that you are in control with your physicality, even if you feel rather frightened.

- Make a note of what has gone on and record the date and time.

- If the situation persists, talk to your manager or to HR.[3]

There is also a website and helpline (National Bullying Helpline), where you will find workplace bullying and harassment dispute specialists who offer employees practical solutions and support.

Sheila White (2013), explores the psychodynamics of workplace bullying and offers some strategies for victims to protect themselves against being bullied again:

1 React faster; don't allow the situation to escalate.

2 Set clear boundaries. Either walk away or explain in a clear and unwavering tone that she or he must stop.

3 Be professional. Don't talk about how you feel, talk about the facts. Rehearse what you are going to say to HR so that you are clear.

4 Seek some help, if you feel traumatized, from a counsellor or therapist.

5 Rewrite your story. When you have been bullied before you may revert to a position of victim: 'Poor me...'. Instead tell the tale of what you would like to happen, with a different outcome.[4]

Bullying and resilience

Dealing with workplace bullying is, as we can see, a different matter from dealing with normal workplace conflict – but that does not mean that developing resilience has no place in how we might handle a severe situation. Professor Andreas Liefooghe (2010), specialist in workplace bullying, describes resilience in this context as increasing one's tolerance for frustration.[5] It may be tempting, accurate and convenient to use a bully–victim narrative when considering a situation – but if you are able, and in a position to – it is perhaps more useful to try and understand the behaviour in context. Resilience can help with this, by allowing us not to jump to the obvious conclusion, to stay with the discomfort and resist the urge to close down complex situations by sticking to a 'them and us' perspective.

Responding to conflict at work

Having explored some of the causes, impacts and different ways that conflict can play out at work, how do we, and can we, respond to it?

The negative lens of conflict

When we explore conflict, it is often with a negative lens. People often view the prospect of conflict with fear and a sense of it being unhelpful; there is certainly a lack of enthusiasm for conflict at work amongst most. Yet we know that conflict of some description at work is inevitable. Research has identified that conflict-induced stress can create physical and psychological problems that can lead to a reduction in productivity, high staff turnover and even burnout.[6] Consequently, dealing with conflict at work in a way that helps people to manage their stress and upset is an imperative.

It is important to note that we deal with conflict in different ways at different times. When we are psychologically strong and secure – when we are resilient – we can deal with challenges and disruption from a secure base, and are less likely to be thrown off course. So our state of mind impacts whether the conflict is a negative experience or a learning experience. We are all also wired differently when it comes to conflict; we have different levels of tolerance for push back or disagreement. For some, only the absolute agreement of every point is acceptable, whereas others are happy to be challenged and questioned and see this as essential to the creative process of working life.

For all of us, though, when we are feeling anxious or pressurized, we can easily slip into unhelpful or dysfunctional behaviour. Thinking about our conflict behaviour can help us to understand the ways in which conflict impacts our resilience. If we are fighters who battle out every difficulty with fire and fury, what consequences might that have on our strength and well-being, not to mention that of our colleagues? Or if we are prone to denial, not acknowledging that issues exist and taking flight from conflict, this might protect us in the short term, but does nothing to build our resilience. Conflict *will* be part of our working experience; it cannot be avoided indefinitely. If we freeze in fear, unable to respond at all as the experience is so unpleasant, we will have no chance to develop our capacity for dealing with conflict situations at work. Facing conflict in a constructive and grounded way gives us the opportunity to build resilience and develop tactics for coping with the next brush with discord.

Typical responses to conflict

There are some typical responses to conflict that we adopt. The Advisory, Conciliation and Arbitration Service (ACAS), which is a public body of the UK Government that sets out to improve working life, has usefully identified these as Fight, Flight, Freeze and Face.

Which one(s) do you identify with?

1 Fight
When faced with a conflict you react in a confrontational way. At work, this may mean shouting or losing your temper. We might know individuals at work who you anticipate 'blowing up' if there is a mistake. They may be feared, and most likely disliked, for unpleasant behaviour when things do not go the way they had hoped or planned. Such individuals might be accused of bullying behaviour, and certainly would not invite constructive dialogue. Passionate objection might also fall into this category of response to conflict, for example when workers feel their rights have been abused or a promise broken.

2 Flight
In flight mode you avoid the problem. This is a common reaction. By discounting a problem, you hope it will go away. Many people in describing their relationship to conflict will say that they simply try and sidestep it. They will turn a blind eye, walk away, tolerate difficulties or make the decision to work differently. It feels stressful and uncomfortable to face up to an ongoing

conflict, whether yours or one between those close to you, so instead you do nothing. This does little to alleviate the situation and can even make it worse.

3 Freeze

In freeze form you are literally unable to react. You are not sure about what you should say or do and you become frozen, you become utterly passive. You might say things like 'I just don't know what to do', or 'I am at a loss.' You can make a conflict last longer than is necessary through your indecision and inability to move matters forward. This can also be a 'rabbit in the headlights' response; we freeze in fear and the consequences can be dangerous for all concerned.

4 Face up to conflict

When we face up to conflict, we approach a problem in a calm and rational way, with a planned approach. We engage with conflict, and in so doing, improve resilience. This is an effective approach. Exercises like Chartier's pin at the end of the chapter may help you work towards this conflict response.

The virtue of workplace conflict – can conflict be helpful?

Some argue that workplace conflict may actually be beneficial; that it could be a catalyst for creativity, problem-solving and demonstrating a willingness to entertain multiple points of view. This is a tempting view to take, but the evidence for the positive outcomes of workplace conflict is really limited, and negative outcomes appear to largely outweigh any positive experience from conflict.[7]

So, tempting as it might be for some, we should resist the urge to view workplace conflict as a blanket 'good thing'. That doesn't mean there can't be positive effects, though – for example, the notion that what remains hidden can be most harmful suggests that conflict can, at times, offer a barometer of organizational health. If fears, loss of trust and animosity remain buried, they will cause individual and team harm. An organization that presents a flawless image is likely to have some resentment and repressed anger below the surface, as presenting this perfect image denies organizations and the people working in them the opportunity to embrace conflict as part of the way they work and develop.

Post-traumatic growth

You've probably heard of post-traumatic stress disorder (PTSD). This is a disorder that develops for some individuals after they have been exposed to a traumatic event – involvement in war, suffering a threat to one's life, an assault etc. After the event, the individual suffers deep mental and physical distress that can incur a number of symptoms, from disturbing thoughts and feelings to an inability to function. The fight/flight response is triggered – this can also cause individuals to bury their trauma, which in turn causes other problems later in life. In a work context, instances of PTSD are less frequent than in a war zone; but assault, fires and even terrorist attacks can all infiltrate working life.

Post-traumatic growth (PTG), on the other hand, is the notion that after the experience of trauma, individuals can benefit from their suffering in some way. For example, they can develop greater resilience. Post-traumatic growth is not a new idea – ancient civilizations and religions have always advocated suffering as a means of yielding a potentially life-transforming experience – but the term 'post-traumatic growth' was coined by the American psychologists Tedeschi and Calhoun in the mid-1990s.[8] Their research showed that as many as 90 per cent of trauma survivors reported at least one element of post-traumatic growth, for example a sense of a renewed appreciation for life.

So how does this fit with the research we mentioned above, that shows the negative outweighs the positive with conflict and trauma? Well, it's important to note that growth is *not* a direct result of the trauma. Instead, work needs to be done to create this growth. Post-traumatic growth reflects the struggle of individuals coming to terms with their new reality after the traumatic event; this is the thing that is crucial in facilitating a growth experience. If we apply this idea to conflict at work, then – by working through conflict, and reflecting afterwards – we can use a negative thing to bring about a positive outcome, and allow ourselves to learn and grow.

There may be other benefits from working through a conflict, too. For example, learning to seek help. Although it is a counter-intuitive way of thinking, negative experiences in the workplace can lead to greater resilience. Even such negative health outcomes as having trouble sleeping or digestive problems can encourage individuals to engage in resilience-promoting behaviour, for example seeking guidance and help.

Promoting resilience in conflict

There are a number of ways in which resilience can be built, enhanced and embedded as a result of conflict. The following ideas may help to embed resilience-promoting conditions.

Sense of control

In a conflict situation resilience will be promoted, or maintained, if you are able to preserve your equilibrium and retain a sense of control. This might look like adjusting to the experience of conflict, and then moving forward in a positive manner; emerging intact, with additional understanding, knowledge and experience.

Listing the issues that need to be dealt with can help you to contain your feelings around the conflict, before then moving on to address the problem. Active problem-solving can also promote resilience when dealing with conflict, as well as helping our sense of well-being and self-efficacy. De Dreu *et al* (2004) found that being involved in the resolution of the difficulties faced led to a greater sense of control and improved health.[9] Dealing with the conflict can have a positive impact on well-being. This can be challenging for some people who hope that problems will simply go away. Facing the conflict can require courage. We may also need to learn how to resolve conflicts and identify different problem-solving techniques.

Speaking up

Feeling isolated and alone is a common complaint amongst those who are involved in a conflict situation. They may feel as if they are not noticed, that their leaders do not care, and that colleagues are simply grateful that they are not the object of attack. So asking for support, or encouraging bystanders to speak up, can be a valuable way of ensuring that unpleasant conflict behaviour that is disrupting performance can be nipped in the bud.

Intervention countering statements that put people down in a way that does not shame the instigator of those statements helps to create a culture of civil and inclusive work behaviour. Here are some examples of what this might look like in practice:

- When you are attacked for a meeting that did not go well with a client and blamed for this you can reply, 'I see that the meeting did not go as you had hoped but it was not only my responsibility. I did prepare for my part of the agenda.'

- If you are accused of being distracted by personal issues when in fact you are dealing with work matters, you can respond simply, 'Actually I am dealing with an important work issue.'

- Perhaps you are criticized for being late again when in fact this is the first time you have been late. You can correct this – 'I value my timekeeping and this is actually a rare occasion owing to a train cancellation (etc).'

This can take courage to do, but clear, factual responses will help to control unhelpful conflict behaviours.

Growing from adversity

The notion of growing from your adversity can help you develop resilience. A study of social workers discovered that resilience was the unexpected outcome of workplace bullying, and that this was particularly so when the person experiencing the bullying was supported by people who witnessed their hardship and by their managers. Turning unpleasant relationships and bullying behaviour into an opportunity to develop strategies to cope can further support resilience in places of work that are conflict-ridden. Although never encouraged or welcomed, here conflict can also help individuals to reframe their experiences and focus on the lessons learned. Van Heugten (2013) cites participants in her research who vowed as a result of their bullying-at-work experiences to be better colleagues and more supportive managers. People in her study displayed resilience in finding opportunities for professional development and personal growth.[10]

Talking

Finding someone that you can talk with about your situation can be a very important and helpful first step. Social support can be vital in working things through and allowing you to release stress and let off steam. Who you choose to talk to is important; try to find a neutral and respected individual who will listen without judgement. When we share our distress, it can be counter-productive to do so with an individual who will add to the negative emotion we are feeling, however tempting it might be. The key is that you want to feel heard, and in talking it through in this way you will also gain clarity about what is troubling you the most.

Mediation and external help

Sometimes it is necessary to call on help outside of the organization and the conflict environment. Mediation is a simple process that allows parties to be heard and gives everyone a chance to air their wounds in a neutral but supportive environment. When you are facing a conflict at work that is stuck, a mediation intervention can help.

A mediator can be used to help resolve disputes, working with all parties in the conflict and allowing broken relationships to be healed. Mediation can be remarkably effective in quickly resolving problems. It is not always helpful of course; both parties have to want the conflict resolved, but it is a largely successful intervention. Mediation may not end every element of the conflict, but it can protect from further damage and set a road map towards fuller resolution. The aim of the intervention is ultimately to reach greater understanding of the situation, hopefully also with greater empathy for the other party's point of view.

Mediation is a voluntary and flexible process. It is also usually conducted in a relatively informal manner. Mediators are facilitators rather than authority figures and this can help all parties to express themselves freely. Mediation is most successful when the parties concerned want to resolve the conflict; this might sound obvious, but many people are invested in their conflicts and do not necessarily want a resolution. It is important that everyone significant participates in the process and is ultimately able to express their reasons for difficulty and angst.

Post-conflict care plan

We know that the brain retains the sense of disruption and alarm caused by conflict for longer than the duration of the conflict itself. So a flare-up at a meeting or a telling-off by our line manager can linger and fester. We can, however, do something to disrupt the way this thinking permeates. Dr Mithu Storoni, author of *Stress Proof* (2019), suggests that we behave in a counter-intuitive way after experiencing a distressing conflict. She advises doing something entirely different that is sufficiently stimulating to occupy our minds but not connected to the conflict. So a challenging puzzle, a yoga session, a game of Tetris – anything that is going to take your mind elsewhere and allow you to focus on some other thing. This will then allow your mind to recover from the distressing conflict and return to a balanced state.[11] Essentially, flopping on the sofa is the worst thing to do, as the feelings of alarm and disruption will stay with us. We need to replace those thoughts with other stimulating thoughts in order to distract ourselves and create a pathway out of our stress.

Focused meditation

Another practice to consider, whether in the midst of conflict or not, is focused meditation. This practice of taking some time out of the working day to quietly engage in focused meditation can reframe your thinking and your state of being. There is guidance at the end of this chapter to help you incorporate this practice into your everyday life. Storoni (2019) promotes the practice as an easy-to-acquire technique that can have a lasting impact.[12]

Finally, it is understandable that when you have experienced conflict or distressing bullying behaviour you feel angry, disrupted and stressed. Yet research has shown that there is a relationship to greater emotional resilience when we embrace forgiveness. Empathy, compassion and sympathy – these responses associated with forgiveness are what will ultimately build our resilience.[13] Forgiveness does not mean that you condone or support the behavior; it allows you to take control, put the conflict behind you and move forward with greater resilience.

Exercises

What is my 'F' response to conflict?

Which description resonates most with how you respond to conflict at work?

Fight

- Do I shout and lose my temper?
- Do I see red?
- Have I been accused of responding aggressively?
- Could this be true?

Flight

- Do I turn a blind eye?
- Do I ignore trouble in the hope it will disappear?

Freeze

- Do I freeze and become passive?
- Do I feel unsure about what to do, so do nothing?

Face up to conflict

- Do I face up to conflict and accept it as inevitable?
- Am I calm and rational?
- Do I engage and learn from the experience?

Focused meditation[14]

This is not classic meditation. This is a quick and easy intervention that can be done anywhere, and involves concentrating on something specific as a way of quieting your internal dialogue. With focused meditation, you still remain in the present moment, but immerse yourself in one thing – whatever that thing may be. It could be a postcard, an image on a mug, a tree that you can see out of the window, the pot-plant on your desk, or a sound or even a smell.

Why is this helpful in building resilience? When we become stressed and worried, we enter a state of mind that impacts not just the isolated event but activities later in the day and beyond. Focused meditation is a way of interrupting that flow of thinking and being and reconfiguring so that we can move forward with fresh thinking. It is simple and can be easily integrated into a working day. Begin with a two-minute session (you can build up to longer periods of time as you become more comfortable).

Steps to follow:

1 Find a quiet spot where your 120 seconds will not be interrupted.

2 Choose the object of your focus.

3 Get comfy, breathe from your belly, loosen your shoulders.

4 Set a two-minute timer on your phone.

5 Turn your attention to your object of focus (picture, mug, tree etc).

6 Don't worry if you get distracted, just gently turn your attention back to your object; you can congratulate yourself for noticing you were distracted.

7 Stay quiet and still – that's it!

Tip: give yourself time to get used to this; we don't usually give something inanimate our undivided attention. Try a few times and see how your practice develops.

Separating the message and the messenger

Separating the individual and their words or actions is a constructive way of dealing with the situation in hand. In so doing we can think of ideas and even behaviours without attaching them entirely to one person, so someone can, for example, do something thoughtless but still be a decent person. Someone could say the wrong thing, but not be a wrong human being. This is about separating the message from the messenger. We can apply this technique to help us manage a conflict at work:

1 Think of the person you are experiencing conflict with.

2 Think of the last thing they said or did to you that caused distress. This might be harsh words or simply a look.

3 Now imagine those same words or non-verbal behaviour from a treasured friend or colleague.

4 Could there be another interpretation?

5 Is it possible that we are experiencing things negatively because we are expecting the worst?

6 Are we unable to separate the message from the messenger?

Chartier's pin

This exercise is designed to help you understand the reason for rude behaviour. The exercise is not to suggest being a pushover, or that we should allow unacceptable actions, but it encourages us to consider how the other person may be feeling. The point is, where it's possible to *understand* rather than simply being offended or hurt, it can help us to avoid descending into rude or angry behavior, too, which can help avoid escalation of a conflict. This concept comes from the French philosopher Emile-Auguste Chartier.

Chartier's pin helps us to understand the motivation behind difficult, unpleasant or even appalling behaviour. Chartier used the case of a pin poking a baby and causing them distress – no matter how one tried to soothe the baby, with food, cuddles, songs, the anguish continued. This was not a fussy or difficult baby. The pin was hurting the infant and nothing would help until the pin was addressed. So when someone behaves badly, it might help to think about what might be causing him or her to act in this way:

- Are they experiencing difficulties in their home life?
- Have they just had a worrying health diagnosis?
- Do they have financial worries?
- Have they recently visited their difficult and cruel family?
- Maybe they do not know how to behave with charm or compassion?

In thinking about their possible 'pin', you can control your response. Rather than reacting with anger or irritation, you can calmly consider what might be behind this behaviour, and move forward.

Going to the balcony

When we are involved in conflict, our emotions are likely to be highly charged. We may be angry, hurt and distressed; we may feel that we have no control. Fisher and Ury, in their seminal text (1981) on dealing with difference, examine the art of negotiation – how to get to an agreement without giving in. Ury asks us to imagine that we are at a distance from our conflict. He invites us to take a position on an imaginary balcony. This position gives us perspective and clarity. It also gives us the chance to calm our emotions and slow down. In suspending our actions and thoughts by viewing our situation from a metaphorical balcony, we have the opportunity to think about what is really important to us. So next time you are involved in a conflict:

1 Take a metaphorical position on the balcony.

2 Count to ten to calm yourself.

3 Look at the conflict situation you are in.

4 Examine what is most important to you.

5 What might it look like from the other person's perspective?

6 Do not rush, and take your time surveying the situation.[15]

Forgiveness

When we have experienced a nasty conflict situation or indeed suffered from an experience of being bullied, the notion of forgiveness might be far from our minds. We may be angry or frustrated, we may feel that we have not been treated well and that we are not understood. We might wish for the perpetrator to acknowledge what they have done wrong, or to be able to make public our suffering, or even for retribution. All of these are understandable responses – yet they are almost certainly ineffective and unhelpful courses of action. The conflict situation has emerged because of a lack of understanding and empathy, after all, so a response that meets your emotional needs is highly unlikely.

Instead you can take control. In a quiet moment and place, imagine you are standing opposite the person that you have been in conflict with. Speak out loud, if you can. Try these steps:

1 This situation has been difficult for me in many ways…
(list what has caused you pain and anguish here).

2 Then write or say out loud, 'I choose to forgive you.'

3 I am sorry this conflict has emerged.

4 I will move forward and not hold on to negative feelings of resentment and anger.

5 Forgiveness will make me stronger.

Endnotes

1 *The Mediator's Handbook* (Beer and Stief, 1997) inspired this model and includes other ways to add to your toolkit in trying to work constructively with difficulties at work

2 Einarsen, S, Hoel, H, Cooper, C (2003) *Bullying and Emotional Abuse in the Workplace: International perspectives in research and practice*, CRC Press, Boca Raton, FL

3 Oade, A (2015) *Free Yourself from Workplace Bullying: Become bully-proof and regain control of your life*, Mint Hall Publishing, Oxford

4 White, S (2013) *The Psychodynamics of Workplace Bullying*, Karnac, London

5 Liefooghe, A P D and Mackenzie Davey, K (2010) The language and organization of bullying at work, *Administrative Theory & Praxis*, 32, pp 71–95

6 Spector, P E and Bruk-Lee, V (2008) Conflict, health, and well-being, https://my.apa.org (archived at https://perma.cc/9GLK-4TD4)

7 De Dreu, C K W (January, 2008) The virtue and vice of workplace conflict: food for (pessimistic) thought, *Journal of Organizational Behavior*, 29 (1), pp 5–18

8 Tedeschi, R G and Calhoun, L G J (1996) The post-traumatic growth inventory: measuring the positive legacy of trauma, *Journal of Traumatic Stress*, 9 (3) pp 455–71, doi:10.1007/BF02103658

9 De Dreu, C K W *et al* (January 2004) Conflict at work and individual well-being, *International Journal of Conflict Management*, 15 (1), pp 6–26

10 Van Heugten K (March, 2013) Resilience as an underexplored outcome of workplace bullying, *Qualitative Health Research*, 23 (3), pp 291–301, https://doi.org/10.1177/1049732312468251 (archived at https://perma.cc/GWT6-3LKD)

11 Storoni, M (2019) *Stress Proof: The ultimate guide to living a stress-free life*, Hodder & Stoughton, London

12 Storoni, M (2019) *Stress Proof: The ultimate guide to living a stress-free life*, Hodder & Stoughton, London

13 Everett, L, Worthington Jr and Scherer, M (2004) Forgiveness is an emotion-focused coping strategy that can reduce health risks and promote health resilience: theory, review, and hypotheses, *Psychology & Health*, **19** (3), pp 385–405, doi:10.1080/0887044042000196674

14 This exercise was informed by an article on www.verywellmind.com (archived at https://perma.cc/2RQN-UGRA) on focused meditation

15 Fisher, R and Ury, W (1981) *Getting to Yes: Negotiating an agreement without giving in*, Random House, Business Books, London

Purpose

As human beings, we want a sense of direction and purpose. This chapter examines the relationship between our purpose, the reason why we work (which is not always the same thing) and resilience. We'll examine the 'why' of resilience, and the importance of purpose in strengthening our resilience.

What is purpose at work?

Purpose expresses a person's sense of resolve. It identifies what we consider to be important and what is worthy of our time. It is our primary task, the thing that we must fulfil. Without fulfilling that purpose we can feel cast afloat without a solid foundation. Work did not used to provide us with this sense of identity, satisfaction and determination; it used to be simply a means to an end, earning enough to live in the way one was accustomed to live. In his 1905 study, the sociologist Max Weber introduced the notion of the Protestant work ethic. This was the turning point when work suddenly became much more about who we were and how we measured our worth.

A sense of purpose is vital to fulfilment and happiness. We've known this about ourselves as a species from the time of the Ancient Greeks, who suggest that it is inherent in human nature to want to do what is worth doing. But what does this mean in a work context? Current thinkers – such as Wharton Professor Adam Grant – show the link between purpose, happiness at work and productivity. Professor Grant has also undertaken studies to show that meaningful work can protect against burnout (2013),[1] so a sense of purpose is important! Stephen Covey (1995) goes so far as to say that a personal mission statement becomes the DNA for every other decision we make.[2]

When your work aligns with your personal values, your sense of purpose can be a key motivator, bringing you improved health and value to your work, supporting your well-being and resilience.

Connect to purpose, connect with others

Purpose motivates and drives us; we connect to our own sense of purpose for a meaningful life, and we connect with others to support the betterment of their life experience. At work, this might look like being a supportive and caring leader, or identifying the development that will support your trainee. Or it could be simply and clearly sharing your vision for work, to help others connect to your reason for working in the way you do. Connected to our purpose, we can be more fulfilled at work, passionate about achieving our goals, and invested in the future of work for us and those around us.

Individual and organizational purpose

When we think about purpose on an organizational level, it can be defined as a way of capturing the essence of the organization as a whole.[3] This means: what the organization is trying to do, why it exists, what difference it makes and to whom. If we're lucky, there is an alignment between our own purpose and that of the organization in which we work. Sometimes this is clear: for example, a surgeon working in a hospital is united with the principles of saving lives and improving the health of patients. Yet how do we ally with our work in human resources if we are employed by a tobacco company? How do we reconcile our principles with our work for a fashion company when we discover it is manufacturing clothes in factories that do not take care of their workers? These are challenging issues.

Simon Sinek has written extensively about the power of finding your purpose. In his book *Start with Why: How great leaders inspire everyone to take action* (2009), he describes purpose as a necessary part of a happy and fulfilling life of a leader at any level. He talks about the what, the how and the why, and stresses that organizations often get embroiled in the what, looking at what can be improved or developed and how that can be done.[4] In so doing, what is lost sight of is the *why* – what drew them and motivated them in the first place.

Purpose at work in practice

Here are some examples from popular culture and society of purpose at work. Oprah Winfrey, who has been enormously successful at capturing the prevalent issues of contemporary society, has recently published her book on purpose, *The Path Made Clear: Discovering your life's direction and purpose* (2019).[5] In it, she urges us to articulate our purpose, to specify what it is we want to achieve:

- What is it I want to achieve?
- Why do I do what I do?
- What am I planning to do with the rest of my working life?

Oprah's manifesto here is to find your purpose and a really clear vision of what you want in life, celebrating along the way. Some other examples might be:

- If we are leading, or working for, the United Nations, our purpose may be to eradicate extreme poverty and hunger, reduce child mortality or create environmental sustainability.

- As individuals we may be driven by smaller but significant goals, such as bringing our passion for self-care to the market (www.selfcarecompany.com); or encouraging people to live well, with more plant-based eating (www. deliciouslyella.com).

- Our aim may be to co-parent our child visibly and without leaving work for long periods.

- If we are suffering from a low point with our mental health, going for a walk every day may well satisfy our purpose.

Why do you go to work?

As we have seen, a sense of purpose at work is an important part of being a happy and resilient worker. So – why do you go to work? It's a vital question when you're considering your own resilience. We're not talking here about the imperative to earn a living to support your needs for food and shelter; we're examining why you go to work at a higher level. Whatever we are pursuing, whatever we are spending our time devoted to, we need to ask an important question: why are we doing this, to what purpose?

How we approach the work we do and the context in which we operate impacts our purpose and our connection to that work. If we're passionate about the work that we're doing, if we care about it at an emotional and at a societal level, we will pursue success in the role – even when there are difficulties.

Here's an example – take the case of a school teacher faced with a reduction in resources, difficult pupil behaviour, changes in legislation and administrative demands. Their resilience in the face of these setbacks will be impacted by their 'why'. Consider the 'why' behind these three professionals:

- Teacher A
  A failed business owner decides to take up primary-school teaching, as the business they were running has lost so much money, they are in debt and they need to earn a salary. The school is local, and the invitation to train and work there is easy.

- Teacher B
  A teacher, the third generation of their family to teach in a primary school, is proud of their vocational history and commitment to

children's education. There is satisfaction in the story of their family history and pride in their role as educators.

- Teacher C
  The third teacher is driven to create the next generation of thoughtful and compassionate citizens. They believe with a passion that the learning and patterns established before senior school are the most significant ingredient in a changed society.

Which teacher is the most resilient to the hardships and challenges of their work? Each of these cases will impact the way in which these teachers work, and the way they cope with setbacks. The stronger the foundations of the 'why', the more centred and strong that individual can be. Although real life is often not as straightforward, this example makes it clear that the third teacher is likely to have the most resilience resources, because their individual purpose is so strongly aligned with the purpose of the school, and their work contributes directly to furthering their personal values. They have a strong awareness of these connections, and all of this will help feed their resilience.

This analysis can be extended to any profession, from professional services like accountancy and the law to public servants such as politicians or government employees; from academics to coffee-shop workers, and artists to small manufacturers. Understanding your purpose can have a profound impact on your resilience, satisfaction and success in working life. With clear purpose and direction, it's much easier to recover from setbacks and continue on your path, because you know where you're going and you have an impetus to continue on that path.

Purpose and the development of resilience

Our sense of purpose can help us develop resilience in the most challenging and dark environment. Victor Frankl's seminal account of the Holocaust, *Man's Search for Meaning* (1959),[6] detailed how he survived the death camps by retaining a sense of purpose in the most terrible of circumstances. His message to the world post-Holocaust was that when there is suffering we cannot necessarily stop that suffering – but we can control how we react to that suffering. For Frankl, the power of purpose was inextricably linked to resilience.

This philosophy is supported by leading cognitive behavioural therapist, Professor Windy Dryden. Dryden (2010)[7] emphasizes the concept of personal responsibility in relation to mental health; that we are responsible for the key areas in our lives that we are able to influence, the things that belong to us, our thoughts and feelings. Times of difficulty, hardship, adversity and challenge are opportunities to develop resilience. Some talk of post-traumatic growth or stress-hardiness; if a person is to grow as a result of hardship, however, they need to have a sense of purpose. One way to think about it would be to say that people need to understand the reason for their suffering, so that it can become a bearable suffering.

We are wired with a strong tendency to hold on to bad experiences and let good experiences pass us by, to literally not allow those good experiences to stick to us. If you have a day at work where everything goes pretty well but one thing is stressful or difficult, that will be the thing that sticks to you. This negativity bias made a lot of sense for our survival in the savannah when we had to be alert to danger; then, that danger meant life or death. It makes less sense in the world of work where inevitably we will be facing challenges on a daily basis, and as we examined in depth, failure is a vital part of a worthwhile working life.

Rings of resilience

When we are clear about why we are doing what we are doing, even if that is exceptionally hard, we have greater resilience. Strongly held values and a deep belief that life is meaningful sit at the core of our purpose: this will give us courage and determination in adversity. Resilience can be triggered if we have a clear purpose – running a marathon in support of a friend in need; working seven days a week to make the start-up you believe in a reality; or campaigning for a cause that sits at the heart of your beliefs, for example. Knowing why we are doing what we are doing will strengthen us, it will help us continue at times of stress and help us bounce back from disappointment and setbacks. As we can see from the figure here, our purpose sits at the centre, and our expression of purpose – our work – follows. Resilience then follows on from that.

Figure 7.1   Rings of resilience

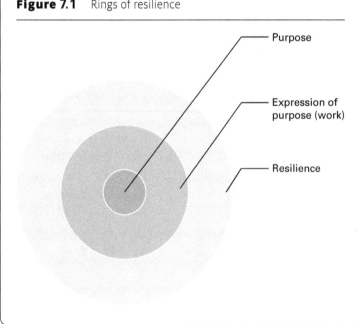

Strong and consistent purpose

Those of us who are fortunate enough to have a strong and consistent purpose, one that touches everything they encounter, are able to use that in a variety of ways. A clearly identified purpose can be used to communicate our needs, identify our priorities, and offer clarity to others about why we are behaving as we are behaving. In turn, this allows us to create a core of resilience, a steel rod that centres us. We are able to continue because we care passionately about what we are doing and want others to understand that.

There are few who have articulated their purpose as eloquently as Martin Luther King Jr, when he conveyed his vision for the American civil rights movement in his iconic 'I have a dream' speech. His dream brought into focus, and made sense of, his campaigning, his speech-making and all his tireless work for equality and the rights of every individual.

We don't always have the opportunity to express our purpose this clearly, because it's sometimes something that we haven't identified that clearly to ourselves – but we can attend to this. At the end of this chapter you will find some exercises that will help you to think about your purpose, what it is that you consider to be your reason for working, the difference you wish to make.

Identity, purpose and resilience

How we define ourselves is linked to our sense of purpose. A receptionist may view their role as vital in building client relationships and being the first impression of the organization, or they may belittle their function as simply answering the phone. A trainee may see themselves as the organization's future, or as the resident low-ranking subordinate who does all the dirty work. Research has been undertaken that links loss of resilience to loss of access to one's identity – and that this access is key to an individual's sense of self.[8] For example, in their work with teachers, Kirk & Wall (2010) found that radical changes in the teaching profession led to issues of confused work and social identity and a subsequent loss of resilience.

The research uncovered that it was not the difficult event itself that caused the participants to feel uneasy and destabilized, but their view of themselves in relation to that event. For example, if they had always seen themselves as someone who coped in disaster situations and they crumbled in a particularly challenging scenario, this was enormously difficult for the individual to face. Pemberton (2015) writes of a newly ascribed identity, of perhaps:

- victim;
- unwanted;
- unprotected;
- vulnerable;
- discounted.

Yet they normally identified with being:

- a winner;
- loved;
- cared for;
- dynamic.[9]

Our personal sense of purpose in this way is not just ascribed to a task or objective or goal, but rather the kind of person we aspire to be. Hopefully, while you have been reading this book, you have had the chance to think about your own relationship to resilience, and to consider the way that adversity features in your life. Perhaps you have even been able to create a fresh identity in the face of future hard times: this is an opportunity to bounce back and redefine yourself as a person of resilience.

From baby boomers to Generation Z

Priorities for different generations will change. Baby boomers born after the Second World War and into the early 1960s expected a certain and fairly traditional career path; Generation X, born between 1965 and 1976, might also have expected some certainty and longevity with one kind of career. On the other hand,

Generation Y (millennials) born between 1977 and 1995, and Generation Z born 1996 onwards, are differently motivated. These latter generations are (generally) used to the unpredictability of work, and to some extent are freer to pursue their dreams. They are unencumbered by traditional expectations, yet burdened by an absence of financial security. For these generations, then, it follows that purpose at work is particularly important.

Purpose and success

Purpose and success are closely linked. What we view as success comes in different forms for different people; we are influenced by the country we live in, the cultural norms we follow, our style, our age and our gender, among other factors. Embracing what success means to each of us with the same understanding that we offer other issues of inclusion and diversity can be incredibly helpful in developing a resilient approach to success.

Although there is no one career path, working pattern, achievement or experience that spells success, there are some common threads. For example, people tend to be happiest when they are utterly absorbed in activities that they find interesting, engaging and meaningful. Where work is neither meaningful nor engaging, we can quickly become disconnected. Psychotherapist and Professor Windy Dryden (2010) emphasizes that meaningful pursuit can not only make you happier, but also improve your mental health. However, he also warns us about the danger of being *so* absorbed that we fail to balance our other life interests. He neatly sums up the balance with this phrase: 'Be devoted, without being devout'.[10] You may be driven to head up a multinational company, or to write a novel, or change the world through good deeds. You may long to lead thousands of people or you may dream of a solitary profession where you can work undisturbed on your research or your project of choice. Whatever your focus, it is healthier to first recognize that this is *your* version of success, and not necessarily the same as those around you, and secondly to remember to maintain a focus on all aspects of your life – not just work. This balance is key for a resilient approach to success.

Purpose around the world[11]

In addition to helping us with resilience, there is evidence that living and working with purpose has benefits, too, for our health and longevity. Helen Russell's work examines the relationship between purpose and happiness. After moving to Denmark, she reflected on the life of the Danes in her book *The Year of Living Danishly* (2016), and found that, rather than fighting for more money at work like people in the UK and the US, the Danes campaigned for more time – time for leisure, for work–life balance and for family. There was also the Danes' notable record of being the happiest country on earth, a record that has been held for decades, as well as their concept of *hygge* or 'cosy time'. It appears that the Danes rank home, friends and family as vital to their purpose, in addition to work, but with the shortest working week in Europe. Russell went on to examine communities around the world that exhibit the longest lives and the greatest happiness. These 'blue zones' are identified and explored in her book *The Atlas of Happiness* (2018). She identifies the cultural beliefs that contribute to happiness through purpose, for example the Chinese who seek their 'xing fu', the thing that gives them real purpose; or the Icelanders whose unwavering belief that all will be well in the end is expressed in their notion of 'petta reddast'.

A life worth living: flow

That common thread to success, whatever your version looks like, has another name: flow. Psychologist Mihaly Csikszentmihalyi identified the state of being when one is engaged utterly and functioning optimally as a state of 'flow' (1992).[12] He began by looking at creative people who spent their life doing something meaningful for them, but that was unlikely to give them either fame or fortune.

What he found is this: when you are absolutely immersed in a process that engages you, there is no attention left over to attend to your bodily needs or your problems at home. The notion of the absent-minded professor may come to mind, the brilliant thinker so focused on the problems to be solved that they forget to get dressed or comb their hair. This flow experience offered Csikszentmihalyi an answer to the question of the secret to happiness.

In his book *Good Business* (2003) Csikszentmihalyi explores leadership flow and the making of meaning. He identifies business leaders nominated by their peers for being not only successful, but also ethical and socially responsible. He defines success here as something that helps others and at the same time makes you feel happy as you are working on it.[13] So work that involves an absorbing challenge and has meaning creates flow. And in flow we are resilient, we are absorbed and we feel a sense of meaningful reward. When was the last time you were in a state of flow? What were you doing? This may give you a clue to your sense of purpose, your idea of success, and how to develop your own resilience.

Positive psychology: PERMA

Martin Seligman is a psychologist who founded a theory called 'positive psychology'. He has written extensively about the potential for a positive human future and the possibility of a flourishing working life. His work with the US Army was a major contribution to this philosophy: in the 2010 Tanner Lectures on Human Values, he describes how he was called to the Pentagon, where he was asked to address the Chief of Staff's concerns about post-traumatic stress disorder (PTSD), suicide, depression, substance abuse and divorce. Seligman offered a more balanced picture of the response of the army to the very real challenges of war. He suggests that reactions to human adversity, rather than being universally negative, are bell-shaped (see figure).[14]

He observed that while a minority of sufferers fell apart, the majority, despite having had a hard time and needing a period of

Figure 7.2 The resilient majority

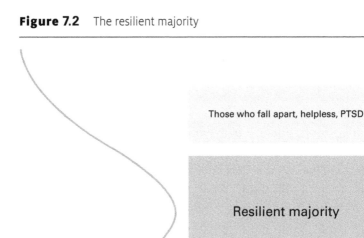

perhaps a few months to restore themselves, were back to where they were according to psychological and physical measures. In addition, he noted that a further minority actually 'bounced forward' – they returned stronger than they were before (post-traumatic growth, which we looked at in the last chapter). His work resulted in the US Army conducting resilience training which covered psychological fitness, social fitness, family fitness and spiritual fitness.

Seligman's work on positive psychology links meaning and the meaningful life. He uses the acronym of PERMA:

- **Positive emotion (P)**
  Viewing experiences through a positive lens in relationships and at work, concentrating on the positive and not dwelling on negative experiences

- **Engagement (E)**
  Absorption in a task, an ability to be fully engaged ('flow')
- **Relationships (R)**
  Building strong relationships to help us thrive
- **Meaning (M)**
  Pursuing meaning rather than wealth or pleasure
- **Accomplishment (A)**
  Goals and ambitions that give us a sense of achievement and attainment

How many of these are fulfilled for you in work?

Finding your purpose

Finding your purpose is not as easy as it sounds. Indeed, people can spend a lifetime in search of meaning. So how do you go about trying to find your own purpose? Derek Draper, in his book *Create Space* (2018),[15] cites the example of the prison officer whose job appeared to be a nightmare – he was poorly paid, worked in a challenging environment and faced constant threats of violence and abuse. He wanted a creative job, one where he found fulfilment, respect and admiration. Yet these are the qualities he ascribed to his job and this was linked to what he saw as his purpose, to save and inspire prisoners and turn them away from a life of crime.

Ikigai

Ikigai is a Japanese concept that means 'a reason for being'. The word is used to offer an indication of the source of value in one's life, basically the things that make life worthwhile. Ikigai suggests we ask ourselves the following four questions:

- What do you love?
- What are you good at?

- What does the world need?
- What can you be paid for?

Answering these key questions and then matching them to our work can help lead to a fulfilling life. Obviously your life is not just about your work; but if we understand our broader purpose, we can then use this as a guiding light for the decisions we make throughout our career.

There is a popular saying that goes: 'Choose a job you love, and you'll never have to work a day in your life.' It's not clear who may have first expressed this idea – but as a sentiment, it has gravitas. If we are working on a task that we feel passionate about, if it aligns with our values and our aspirations, then work is far less of a drudge and far more about satisfaction and even joy. Being guided by the principles of Ikigai can help us with a clear sense of focus and stability when we are facing crossroads in our careers or have doubts about what direction to take. Having a greater sense of purpose can lead to greater mental and physical well-being.

Avoid self-blame

Self-blame is a destructive activity and should be redirected to self-care, thinking about how we can take better care of ourselves. Being well rested and restoring yourself can help you to deal with the demands of work and home. Self-care is essential for a healthy work–life balance. For example, you need time to switch off, we cannot be working effectively all the time. Interventions are possible that create both physical and psychological fitness.[16] At the end of this chapter there is an exercise entitled 'Three good things': this is a practice that encourages us to examine what has gone well for us and to redirect our thinking to what is good. Gratitude as a practice has been found to have a hugely positive impact on our well-being. Such interventions can build our long-term resilience capability.

With more self-care and less self-blame, we can turn down the volume of our inner critic. We might not be able to switch it off completely, but we can make the noise less disruptive. And we can also adopt a position of 'self-celebration' for the things that have gone really well for us, too. We are quick to accuse ourselves of being the author of various misdemeanours and downfalls, but we are generally far more reluctant to take credit for what we have done well. Being resilient means not only forgiving ourselves for what might not have gone perfectly, but having the strength to acknowledge the times when what we have done is really very good.

Working life is hard and demanding. It can be challenging to switch off from work and it can be easy to feel guilty when you are not working. When demands become unrealistic and unreasonable, we can quickly blame ourselves and not recognize that it is actually unattainable to work under such pressures. Such self-stigmatization can make us feel hopeless and have a negative impact on our long-term goals and well-being.[17]

Purpose and courage

Committing to a working life of purpose takes courage. It may mean that your path is not the one expected of you by family, friends and peers. It might mean making choices that surprise people close to you. Yet only *you* can decide what really matters to you. We have a finite working life, and finding and working with your chosen path is an opportunity not to be overlooked.

Some people might think it is too late to change in their twenties, while others are bounding for new adventures in their eighties. Our purpose may change throughout our working lives, and it's never too late to explore that change. Answering the question 'what do I want to do with my working life?' and attempting to align your personal goals and your professional goals may not be easy, but doing so will offer you the opportunity to have a working life of meaning and purpose.

Exercises

Shine a light on your purpose

Have a go at some of these creative approaches to defining your purpose:

Purpose press release

To help you to connect with the purpose of the work that you are doing, and that of your organization, write a press release that sums up what you offer the world. What is it that is contributing to the greater good of the world, the things that make getting up and going to work worthwhile, the things that make the difficulties at work meaningful?

Tweet

Use 144 characters to share the same message.

Induction

Imagine that you are your manager, and you are hiring yourself. Tell this new member of staff (you!) who has joined your team what their contribution means. What are the top three points you want to share?

1

2

3

In six words – what is your purpose at work?

We can have any number of tasks that we perform that are useful and part of our pattern of working life. But why are we doing all these things? What is our purpose at work? This can be functional – we need to earn money to pay the rent, for example – or it could be that we are connected to a higher purpose, one that makes a difference in this world. This exercise forces you to channel your thinking about your purpose into just six words. Here are some examples:

My purpose is to: Contribute, stimulate and challenge.

My purpose is to: Use my creativity for change.

My purpose is to: Raise awareness of environmental damage.

How do you describe your purpose in six words?

My purpose is to:

_____

Three good things[18]

Linking well-being to purpose, this exercise encourages you to firstly think about what is good for you, and then what is the thing that you define as meaningful. What have you done that links to the greater good, and in service of a meaningful life?

See if you can commit to repeating this exercise once a day for a week. Before you go to sleep write down three good things that went well today:

1

2

3

Think about why those things went well.

Finding your flow

Flow is identified as a way of working that reflects your peak performance. You are involved in tasks that are meaningful to you and that offer you a meaningful reward. Think of a time when you were engaged in work and felt you were being your 'best self'. Write an account of your peak experience, answering some or all of the following questions:

1 What attracted you to the piece of work?

2 Why was it challenging?

3 Why was it meaningful to you?

4 Who else was involved?

5 How did you deal with difficulties you encountered?

6 How did you stay motivated?

7 How did you celebrate your success?

Thinking about these issues will help you to identify your own peak flow conditions. Remember they may be different for everyone. It can help you identify why you are in difficulty at times of stress, when you are not in flow.

Investigating Ikigai

Ikigai is the Japanese concept that means 'a reason for being'. What is the essence of what makes your life worthwhile? Ask yourself the following key questions:

1 What do I love?

2 What am I good at?

3 What does the world need?

4 What can I be paid for?

Try answering these questions in a Venn diagram. Is there any overlap?

Figure 7.3   Ikigai Venn diagram

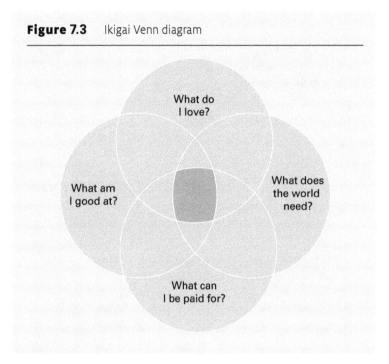

Endnotes

1 Grant, A (2013) *Give and Take: A revolutionary approach to success*, Weidenfeld & Nicolson, London

2 Covey, S R, Merrill A R, Merrill R R (1995) *First Things First*, Simon and Schuster, New York

3 Obholzer, A and Roberts, V Z (2019) *The Unconscious at Work: A Tavistock approach to making sense of organizational life*, Karnac, London

4 Sinek, S (2009) *Start with Why: How great leaders inspire everyone to take action*, Penguin, London

5 Winfrey, O (2019) *The Path Made Clear: Discovering your life's direction and purpose*, Bluebird, London

6 Frankl, V E (1959) *Man's Search for Meaning*, Rider Books, London

7 Dryden, W (2010) *10 Steps to Positive Living*, Orient Paperbacks, Delhi

8 Kirk, J and Wall, C (2010) Resilience and loss in work identities: a narrative analysis of some retired teachers' work-life histories, *British Educational Research Journal*, 36 (10), pp 627–41

9 Pemberton, C (2015) *Resilience: A practice guide for coaches*, Oxford University Press, Oxford

10 Dryden, W (2010) *10 Steps to Positive Living*, Orient Paperbacks, Delhi

11 Russell, H (2016) *The Year of Living Danishly*, Icon, London; (2018) *The Atlas of Happiness: The global secrets of how to be happy*, Hodder & Stoughton, London

12 Csikszentmihalyi, M (1992) *The Psychology of Happiness*, Rider, London

13 Csikszentmihalyi, M (2003) *Good Business: Leadership flow and the making of meaning*, Viking Penguin, London

14 Seligman, M (2010) *Flourish: Positive psychology and positive interventions*, The Tanner Lectures on Human Values, delivered at The University of Michigan, https://tannerlectures.utah.edu/documents/a-to-z/s/Seligman_10.pdf (archived at https://perma.cc/M99A-8NYC)

15 Draper, D (2018) *Create Space: How to manage time, and find focus, productivity and success*, Profile Books, London

16 Seligman, M (2010) *Flourish: Positive psychology and positive interventions*, The Tanner Lectures on Human Values, delivered at The University of Michigan, https://tannerlectures.utah.edu/documents/a-to-z/s/Seligman_10.pdf (archived at https://perma.cc/M99A-8NYC)

17 Corrigan, P W, Larson, J E and Ruesch, N (2009) Self-stigma and the 'why try' effect: impact on life goals and evidence-based practices, *World Psychiatry*, 8 (2), pp 75–81

18 This exercise is adapted from Martin Seligman's work on *Positive Psychology*. In his work he found that when people do an exercise like this one for six months, they report feeling less depressed and have higher positive emotions than a placebo group. Gratitude is a practice that has been found to have a hugely positive impact on our well-being (2010 Tanner Lectures)

08
Closing thoughts

We began this book with an examination of the way in which the circumstances of our work have changed dramatically. Our expectations of workplaces, work colleagues, structure, technology, communication, tasks, availability and skill have all been transformed. And our resilience has been tested as a result. We have also explored how in every area of our working life, and in the self we bring to work, we have an opportunity to work with that experience, to take some risks, to experience failure and ultimately to learn.

It is hard to compare our style of work with that of the bleak working conditions of the working classes in the industrial north of England before the Second World War. These conditions were vividly captured by the writer George Orwell in his 1937 book, *The Road to Wigan Pier*.[1] He describes the back-breaking 'commute' of miners who had to crawl through tunnels to get to the coalface where they carried out their seven and a half hours' work, before crawling back again to the lift and daylight. The time spent crawling in the dark was not paid, and getting to work was like climbing a small mountain at the beginning and end of every gruelling working day. Our work challenges are all-encompassing; but they are rarely as physically demanding as Orwell describes. The challenges we face are largely psychological.

In this final chapter I leave you with some thoughts and suggestions that relate to each of the topics we have worked through. In it I encourage you to adopt an attitude of curiosity, kindness and gratitude to yourself and your circumstances. There are so many occasions when we berate ourselves for our failures and for not performing at our best. But adopting such a mindset can create a punitive internal space, which punishes failure and leaves little room for kindness and self-compassion.

Remembering your potential for resilience

It takes time and practice to develop a new skill. Resilience is no different. When you next encounter something that is threatening or upsetting – pause. There is great power in the pause. It gives us time to adopt our new response and shift our perspective. Our first reactions are not always the most helpful. We can react with hurt, disappointment, anger, frustration and surprise. It's important to take time to reflect on the disappointment we have experienced, to put it into context, to imagine what else might be going on. Decisions are nuanced; there is little that is simply right or wrong, there are shades of light and dark. It is OK to acknowledge your disappointments, but you should also try to acknowledge your achievements.

Think of a difficult situation or challenge that you have faced – perhaps you were overlooked for promotion, for example – and see how you can adjust your thinking:

Figure 8.1   Resilient frame of mind

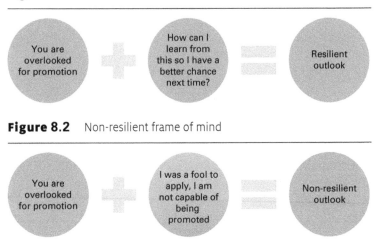

Figure 8.2   Non-resilient frame of mind

Shifting your outlook from a non-resilient frame of mind to a resilient frame of mind is not necessarily easy, as we have seen. We require a different way of thinking and the willingness to bring this mentality into the everyday. Here are some more examples of other situations you may face at work:

- Failing a professional examination

  - The outlook of a resilient person might be: 'My learning is not lost. What else do I need to do in order to have a better chance of passing next time? It is within my reach, and the sting of not passing first time will fade once I have achieved my qualification.'

  - The non-resilient mentality may respond: 'I can't put myself through that again, I tried hard and I failed, I won't do that again, I am not able to pass. I was a fool to apply, I will never be qualified, as I am not capable.'

- You are not shortlisted for a job that you imagined was perfect for you

  - The mindset of a resilient person responds: 'I am disappointed but I know how much I wanted this job. Where else might I look to find a similar opportunity? What can I do to develop myself so that I have a better chance next time I apply? What did I learn from this disappointment?'

  - The non-resilient mindset counters: 'I was wrong. If it had been just right they would have appointed me. Maybe I am not right to look for a job like this.'

- Your presentation is publicly criticised by your manager

  - The mindset of a resilient person might go: 'This feedback is helpful; I can use this perspective to help me create an even better presentation next time. I have added to my knowledge.'

  - A non-resilient mindset can be brutal: 'I am an idiot, I missed certain facts, it was all terrible, I won't present again.'

The last example hints at the self-destructive behaviour we can direct towards ourselves when we are unforgiving of our setbacks and limitations. Regularly reminding yourself to be kind to yourself is not indulgent; it is sensible, it is human.

Learned resilience

In Chapter 1, we examined failing and the impact of positive psychology on the way we view failure. Learned helplessness is a term coined by the positive psychologist Martin Seligman, following a series of animal experiments in 1972.[2] Notwithstanding the ethics of such experiments, the Pavlovian responses uncovered teach us something valuable in relation to resilience.

In these experiments, dogs had previously endured repeatedly painful stimuli which they were unable to escape or avoid. When placed in a new situation – one where these painful stimuli *could* be avoided – the dogs did not do so.

In other words: because they had been *unable* to avoid something in the past, they failed to explore options to avoid this unpleasantness in new circumstances. They didn't escape because they were conditioned to believe that they could not, even though it was easy, even though it just took a small leap. Seligman applied this pattern of thought to those who teach themselves that they are helpless, because in a previous role they were and imagine that they will be similarly helpless in new circumstances.

What do we teach ourselves we cannot do at work? Do we decide that because we struggled with delegating tasks when we were first promoted that we are now not a good delegator? Or that because we became over-emotional when we had to convey some bad news at work, we are not to be trusted with matters of sensitivity? If you took a step back and reflected on your 'learned' helplessness at work, what would that mean for you?

In addition to learned helplessness, Seligman also wrote about learned optimism (1990).[3] He described the arrival at optimism as being a journey, where emphasis is first placed on understanding

Figure 8.3   Learned helplessness and learned resilience

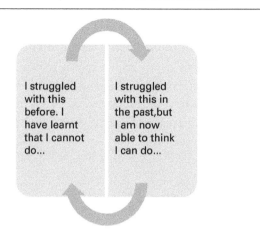

your current state of mind and response to events, be that an immediately positive or negative experience, and exploring alternatives. We can apply similar thinking to resilience. We may think of ourselves as a fragile individual with little internal resilience, yet reframing our experiences can allow us to develop a more resilient mindset. The RAS Affirmations exercise at the end of the chapter will support you in reframing your sense of self.

Situational resilience

The context in which we operate can have a significant impact on our resilience. If we are feeling safe and supported it might be easier to take a risk, challenge an instruction or think creatively. The notion of containment that we examined in some depth in Chapter 5 emphasized the potential of working within the boundaries of this inspiring but safe space. It is easy to delegate that responsibility to those who manage and lead us; you might think of examples of great leadership where people are empowered to be the very best versions of themselves. Creating that inner psychological space and shifting our internal locus of control, so that we can face life events without falling into troubling patterns of behaviour, is the ultimate tool of resilience. It is creating autonomy of resilience. We do not have to depend on our leaders, our colleagues or our clients to create the right circumstances in which we can flourish; we can take charge of that with self-care and attending to what we need.

Resilience is hard to grasp; whether you have it or not depends on where you are in your life, how your life is unfolding and the key challenges and events that you have to work through. We can be crushed or we can rise up.

Learning from others

When we receive feedback, it can be hard to hear what is being identified. If we are sensitive or feeling vulnerable, rather than hearing: 'Your presentation was a bit dull,' we hear 'YOU are a bit dull.' When we are told that our report requires further work, rather than taking on board 'I think you need to look deeper into these issues,' we might hear 'I'M not clever, I'M shallow.' This is faulty thinking.

Eleanor Roosevelt famously said that no one can make you feel inferior without your permission. Take this thinking into your working life. Think of a time when you felt belittled or upset at work. The way you act is in your hands. If you feel humiliated or made to look foolish, you can act graciously. You can accept that, from the other person's perspective, things haven't gone well. You can accept their comments. You can outwardly deal with the communication.

There was a favoured construction in management training in the past that encouraged the use of a 'feedback sandwich': whatever development issue you wanted to identify should be sandwiched between two positive observations or pieces of praise. It became colloquially known as the 's**t sandwich', and didn't quite work the way it was intended. The receiver tended to overlook any positive observations and focus solely on the sandwich filling of criticism. A more candid approach than this might be to make clear

Figure 8.4   Faulty thinking

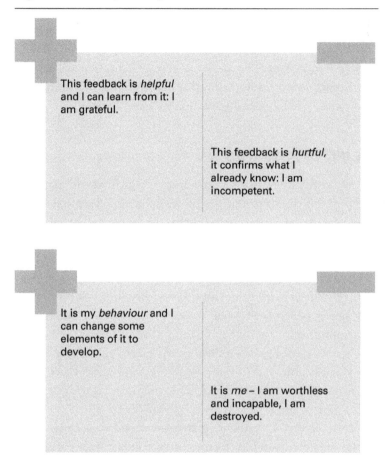

This feedback is *helpful* and I can learn from it: I am grateful.

This feedback is *hurtful,* it confirms what I already know: I am incompetent.

It is my *behaviour* and I can change some elements of it to develop.

It is *me* – I am worthless and incapable, I am destroyed.

that you have some feedback, to check if the person is willing to receive it, to be clear and specific and then to discuss what might be done to address the issue constructively. Don't try to disguise the feedback.

Sheryl Sandberg (2017)[4] advocates another layer to the feedback process, which encourages us to interrogate ourselves about how we responded to the piece of feedback. She cites the law professors Stone and Heen who propose a self-assessment of how you respond to feedback. There is an exercise that builds on that at the end of the chapter. Exercising our ability to listen and respond to feedback without feeling crushed by it is an excellent skill that can be transferred from any job to another, as a leader, a follower or as a colleague. This additional layer to the feedback process can also allow you to look at the experience from a slight distance, to witness yourself and consider 'How did I deal with that observation in the meeting?', 'What was my reaction to that suggestion?'

The gift of feedback

Not all feedback is delivered in a way in which we are ready to receive it; this can have much to do with the messenger and much to do with the receiver. Brené Brown, the courage guru, offers a checklist (2018)[5] to measure how engaged we are and how ready we are to receive feedback: are we in a state of readiness to receive? This involves self-reflection and an honesty about mutual acceptance, a readiness to listen and an acknowledgement that resolution of whatever issue or challenge we are facing will lead to growth and opportunity.

When someone has taken the time to observe you closely, to see how you perform, and to understand the ways in which you are experienced, and then share that with you, it is a gift. It demonstrates interest and a focus on your growth.

Not all feedback is about improvement and development, of course: some feedback also focuses on recognition. Our purpose is enhanced when we are recognized for our contribution. A Nobel Prize is an international and prestigious recognition – but a thank you from a satisfied customer can also be incredibly meaningful. There is wonderful value in feeling that your work has purpose, and that you are also seen to be doing something meaningful to others. There is, moreover, a strong correlation between resilience and the maintenance of self-perception. So tell those around you that you would value hearing when things have gone well. Competent and successful people are assumed to know that they are such. Take responsibility – it is in your hands.

Self-blame to self-care

We have explored the many potential and deep-seated reasons for our tendency to blame ourselves when things go wrong in Chapter 3. Self-blame is a destructive activity and should be redirected to self-care – thinking about how we can take better care of ourselves. Being well rested and restoring yourself can help you to deal with the demands of work and home. Gratitude is a practice that has been found to have a hugely positive impact on our well-being.

Authenticity is important to note here. Investigations into the military suggest that false bravado, the attempt to deny stress and trauma, can encourage people to 'fake good' until they actually collapse. This 'putting a brave face on it' might be taught under the banner of resilience... but has little to do with an *authentic* resilience. Through developing self-awareness and self-knowledge we can understand better when we are in a vulnerable state and when we need to ask for support to deal with difficulties.

When you are feeling hugely pressured at work, find the courage to talk to your manager and explain that you are overstretched. And if you are the manager, perhaps have that conversation before things get to that stage, by making it known that your reports can talk to you if there are changes needed to better structure the workload.

Sometimes we are experiencing issues that cannot be dealt with at work. When we face these outside challenges we need to seek support, guidance and comfort from experts who can guide us to the help we need.

Forgive yourself your failures

Failure has become the topic *du jour*. It has always been a condition – fear of failure even has a name: 'atychiphobia', the irrational and persistent fear of failing. But recently, there has been a shift in the way failure is viewed. The excellent podcast series by Elizabeth

Day, *How to Fail*, showed that a life lived to its fullest is one that will be littered with failures. She interviewed a range of successful celebrities who shared their own experiences of failure. This became a book of the same name, which captured the essence of a more honest and multidimensional existence – one that's sometimes glossed over in social media and in soundbites. Day advocates that failure is part of living life amply, living in technicolour.[6] A similar theme is dealt with in the searingly honest and gutsy *The Art of Not Falling Apart*, in which Christine Patterson (2018)[7] tackles the ups and downs of life, including when your identity is crushed through redundancy. In her reflections on failure in her autobiography *Becoming* (2018)[8] Michelle Obama urges us not to be afraid to fail, recognizing that it is an essential part of growth and development.

Failure might not be our first-choice outcome; it might be that we are dealing with *Option B* as described in the recent book by Sheryl Sandberg and Professor Adam Grant (2017).[9] But as resilient creatures we now know that we can recover from our failures, and we can make the best of things.

Learn from your mistakes

There is a new terminology emerging about parents who are so overprotective that they plan ahead in great detail to avoid their offspring facing any difficulty, literally smoothing their paths so that they can glide through daily life without upset. It could mean that a child frightened of animals is not allowed to go to a party if the family has a pet, or the family are instructed to remove the pet from the house. Or it might mean a parent providing a detailed list of likes and dislikes about their child's food preferences. This is colloquially called 'snowploughing' – 'shovelling' anything that gets in the way out of sight. And whilst well-intentioned, this robs the child of the chance to discover who they really are, a discovery that comes only from learning to trust yourself, from making mistakes and learning from them.

At work, this kind of well-meaning sheltering can mean our first encounters with adversity feel brutal. And if we are leading in such a way that prevents our team from learning, we are also doing those who work for us a disservice. Spoon-feeding instructions and directing detailed behaviour will rob the people who work with you of the chance to develop their own strength and ability.

Another accusation hurled at parents of the so-called 'snowflake generation' is that of 'helicopter parenting'. This involves managing children's lives so closely that there is no potential for independence and the creation of a sense of self borne from one's own decisions and experience. Here we encounter the first cousin of resilience: grit. Charles Murray, the author of *The Bell Curve* (1994),[10] describes this rather harshly: without grit, students will have the resilience of brittle champagne flutes. This vivid description of an easily shattered body, only useful in a rarified environment and with a need to be handled very carefully, seems to offer a stifled existence and great limitations on the potential of work.

Aristotle named tenacity as a key virtue, and perseverance is critical in overcoming our failures. Although Gladwell's exploration of success in *Outliers* (2008)[11] identified luck, he also named perseverance and practice as vital tools – in his well-known definition, it takes 10,000 hours of perseverance to reach excellence. Angela Duckworth's research and subsequent book (2017)[12] on the importance of grit in success, above talent, reinforce the message of this book. You have to be willing to fail and then to begin again; to know that failure is not a permanent condition.

Find your tribe

A key life lesson is the acceptance that we will not be liked by everyone. At work, there will be dynamics, agendas, insecurity and ambition. Knowing that there will not be universal approval for your ideas or plans requires resilience. We need to accept that in the complex web of work there will be diversity of opinion and diversity of affection – but the crucial part is knowing that this does not mean that we are not likeable; this does not mean we have failed. Finding the supportive network that you can turn to for guidance and space to explore ideas will help to balance your sense of what you are contributing.

Liberating yourself from the notion of pleasing everyone or being liked by everyone can free up space to focus on things that are important to you. It doesn't mean that you should be unpleasant or go out of your way to adopt unpopular decisions, but simply to accept that at times there will be decisions you make that won't be universally liked. This will have the added benefit of making you worry less. You will also have more time to focus on work and the projects that matter most to you.

The ABC of resilience

Research into resilience is relatively new, and a great deal of the early work placed emphasis on the negative impact of life events such as trauma or hardship. Garmezy (1990, 1993)[13] was one of the first to recognize that there is an alternative perspective. He investigated what allows some people to cope with negative events and bounce back from challenging life events and what makes others crumble. What protective factors might be at play? An examination of how resilience works offers some emergent themes.[14] Those who are resilient:

Accept their reality;

Believe that life has meaning;

Have an ability to Change and improvise.

Throughout this book we have looked at the need to accept ourselves, our failures and our working reality. We tackled the relationship of resilience to purpose in Chapter 7 and the particular challenges of change, loss and disruption in Chapter 4.

In a *Harvard Business Review* examination of *How Resilience Works* (2002)[15] the ability to change and improvise is named as 'ritualized ingenuity' or 'bricolage'. Claude Lévi-Strauss, the French anthropologist, brought us this notion as both a method of inventiveness and a means of making something from a collection of unrelated things. In French, *bricolage* means 'DIY', or 'home repairs'. This can be a helpful idea when considering resilience – we might not *choose* to take on a different role, or work without our usual resources, or when we are unwell or frail, but in so doing we might discover a new way of working, a new solution to an existing problem.

A case of ingenuity, loss and renewal

Maya Shankar was a gifted child musician with a trajectory to remarkable success as a violinist. She practised for hours, anticipated only a musical career, and devoted everything to this end with great success. She was mentored by Itzhak Perlman, and became a student at the prestigious music academy the Juilliard. An unexpected injury closed that possibility, her dream ended and with it a crushing loss of an imagined career and purpose. Maya had to rethink her life and purpose. She went on to become a social scientist, a White House Advisor, Chair of a Social & Behavioural Team, and the first Behavioural Science Advisor to the United Nations. She is now Head of Behavioural Insights at Google.[16]

Difference and the puzzle of resilience

It is important to emphasize something we witness constantly; that there is a difference in the ways in which people respond to challenges and adversity, and the ways in which they act with resilience. We examined the unique nature of our human experience in Chapter 3, and the below-the-surface dynamics that influence the relationship we have with ourselves and others. We now know that what causes an existential crisis in one person may be hardly noticed by another.

There is also a temporal issue at play – we may be remarkably resilient in our twenties, fragile in our thirties, strong again in our forties, but frail in our fifties. These changes need not occur over decades; it could be day-to-day, week-to-week, month-to-month. Our relationship to resilience is not static.

And there can be gender differences too. Work by the Failure Institute[17] has shown that when men set up businesses that fail, they tend to quickly move on to another venture, perhaps in a slightly different sector. When women fail they may take their time, possibly impacted by the notion of imposter syndrome. Women's resilience is also influenced by hormones, menopause and pregnancy, and men face enormous pressures to be powerful and have to work harder to be accepted at an emotional level, although these paradigms are slowly changing. Yet what is striking is that there *are* different assumptions made about the same failure.

Age can impact our resilience. We should be wary of stereotypes, but also conscious that how old we are may play a factor in our resilience. As young members of the workforce we can bring enthusiasm, an ease with digital communication and technology, an open mind to possibilities. These qualities can allow us to embrace challenges with fresh insights, energy and optimism. Those who have been working for many years bring with them experience, but they are likely, too, to bring a learnt way of dealing with problems that might not be right for the current and present challenge. Perhaps the way that they have always dealt with issues is no longer appropriate or the best fit for the problem that work brings. Of course, there are also the lessons learnt that accompany our maturity, the experience that teaches us that 'this too shall pass' and perhaps a growing recognition of our potential.

There is no even playing field at work, in the same way that there is difference and inequality in life. Social and economic status, race, health, ability and disability create complexities, and the relationship to resilience of all the factors of difference identified remain a puzzle; we do not know the answer to why some are more resilient than others.[18]

Does privilege create an absence of resilience? Do power dynamics force those without power to become more resilient? These are all questions that cannot be answered with certainty.

Bounce back, bounce forwards

Some would argue with the very notion of bouncing back. They would see it as a regressive step, believing that part of the journey to resilience involves a recognition that we are never the same after a difficult or challenging experience – we may *appear* to be the same, but our knowledge, self and experience are changed, often for the better.

Greitens (2015),[19] in examining what hardship, suffering and pain can offer us, pushes against the notion of resilience as a bouncing back to what was before, in an elastic sense. A former Navy SEAL, his examination of resilience in a series of letters to a colleague of his (a veteran struggling with PTSD) shows how we can build purpose and confront pain – emerging differently from the experience, more knowledgeable, understanding and compassionate.

We can compare this to the Japanese art of Kintsugi, or the art of precious scars. Kintsugi is a way of embracing the flawed or the imperfect, valuing the marks of wear and tear on a vessel. This traditional method uses a precious metal, often gold or silver, to bring together pieces of broken pottery. In repairing what is broken something even more lovely is created. From the damaged pottery something enhanced and elevated emerges. The cracks and repairs are events in the life of an object and the repair is illuminated.

So, too, with our own scars, visible or hidden, that express the vicissitudes of life with all its knocks and breakpoints. This book has given you tools to help you flourish at work. You will now be aware that resilience can be taught. There are ghosts of our past that whisper to the child within the adult.[20] But you can heal your wounds and move on. You can bounce back – or bounce forwards.

As we progress through key changes in our life and career, there is a notion of 'a new normal' when we occupy new positions and new roles. These are not just physical functions such as a promotion, a fresh place of work or a change of career; we can also occupy the new normal of a different place of psychological understanding, bouncing back to a new place, with increased self-knowledge, understanding and strength. I look forward to hearing your stories of how you have bounced back, from failure and challenges and how your resilience has grown.

What we have learnt

During this book we have discussed taking care of our brain and our body. An interest in the interconnectedness of mind and body is emerging. There is a recognition that we need to take care of ourselves holistically. Those who know this – neuroscientists – embrace yoga and running. The success of Dr Rangan Chatterjee's podcast *Feel Better, Live More* and his books (2017, 2018),[21] which urge a four-pronged approach to relax, eat, move and sleep our way to a healthier life, are examples of this shift – our behaviour can change our mood.

And there is so much to discover below the surface. Developing our self-awareness will help us to recognize what our triggers are and give us space to examine our unhelpful behaviours, to be gentle with ourselves. Consider this as a self-assessment, a due diligence of you. This is a lifelong task. We have also considered the inevitable change, disruption and loss that we will encounter during our working lives, and that, in a Stoic sense, we should prepare for this and embrace the experiences on offer.

Whether we are leaders or followers, there will be a special call on our resilience, as expectations on both sides are expressed and we learn to develop our style and way of working. There will be conflict and disagreements, relationships that are tricky to deal with and people who will challenge us.

What is yours to cherish when everything else is stripped away? Deciding what is important to you and what you want to achieve will bring meaning to your time at work, pleasure, satisfaction and development. And yet in all these areas of work you will fail and make mistakes, forgive yourself and learn from it.

You will fail again.

You will bounce back.

It is now time to focus on what you can do to build your resilience.

That's all I have for now – good luck.

Exercises

Quick fixes when your resilience drops

For yourself:

- Go outside.
- Take a brisk walk and get some fresh air.
- Write a list of concerns.
- Find someone supportive to speak to.
- Find somewhere private and take some deep breaths.

For those around you:

If you notice someone is agitated or distressed, help them to get through their struggle by removing them from the situation that is stressing them, for example by asking them if they want to step out of the office, or offer them a cup of tea and a chance to discuss their immediate worries.

RAS affirmations

Affirmations are an easy and adaptable way in which to encourage movement and redefinition. They can be used to create a new way of looking at yourself, but also reinforce those elements of your psychological self that are already helpful and that you want to keep. Here's how: the Reticular Activating System (RAS) – a name for one of the many functions of the brain – makes regularly repeated words part of our identity. This means that if we continually call ourselves stupid, we will identify as stupid; if we continually call ourselves bright, we will identify as bright. The RAS sits at the base of our brain, and acts as something of a filter for all the millions of bits of information and data that surround us. For the purposes of this exercise we can also think of the RAS as our Resilience Activation System.

Our minds do not know the difference between past and future; for the brain, it's all about the here and now. It is important to state your affirmation in the present tense. If you practise affirmations regularly, they will start to form part of your identity.

In this exercise you will find a list of suggested affirmations that can support your road to resilience; but there may be other, more appropriate, affirmations that you define. Find what works for you.

Begin by saying the affirmations out loud as you look in the mirror. If it is too difficult and uncomfortable to look at yourself as you say these affirmations, just say them out loud. If you have a bathroom cabinet, you could affix the list inside to remind you to make this practice as routine as brushing your teeth. It might feel rather odd at first – but you will get used to the practice if you keep it up. Every day, repeat your chosen affirmations, and slowly they will feel part of your identity.

RAS affirmations

What you focus on most will be what you identify as, so focus on this: *I am resilient. I can bounce back.*

1 It's OK, I can do this.

2 This is enough. It may not be perfect but it is good enough.

3 I am ready to listen and learn and improve my understanding.

4 If I fail, it is not the end; what did I learn?

5 If I failed, I can try again.

6 I have hidden resources of strength.

7 Negative committee that meets in my head – sit down and shut up!

8 I can accept my new circumstances, even if it is not what I imagined.

9 I do not have to stay in my comfort zone.

10 If I face a bump, I can bounce back.

Add to this list as you face new challenges.

Identifying your coping strategies

We all have existing ways of coping with stress and difficulty. Some of these activities will support the development of greater resilience, while some may be destructive. Be gentle with yourself, and begin to examine your coping strategies. What else could you do to move to a more constructive way of building your resilience and bouncing back?

Here are some common coping strategies. Which ones do you default to? Which ones would you like to include in your personal resilience toolkit?

- **Acceptance**
  You acknowledge that this is a difficult period, that you are struggling, that something needs to change.

- **Active coping**
  You seek help to support your stress, engage in meditation, relaxation techniques, therapeutic intervention, essentially doing something constructive to support yourself.

- **Behavioural disengagement**
  You turn away from situations that distress, reducing eye contact, not engaging with others, demonstrating your restlessness, stress or boredom through your body language.

- **Humour**
  When you are laughing it is hard to feel like a victim. Reframing tragic or challenging situations with humour can help shift from one strategy to the next.

- **Planning**
  Planning for adversity can help you feel better prepared when troubles strike; knowing what steps you can take to recover can improve resilience.

- **Positive reframing**
  You reconsider facts in a positive light as a way to transform your thinking (see also the exercises at the end of the conflict chapter).

- **Religion**
  Those with faith may find greater capacity to deal with adversity when there is a sense of greater good, a greater power directing events that are experienced as difficult.

- **Self-distraction**
  Finding ways of doing other things that distract you from conflict, upset, stress or upsetting emotions is a useful tool in building self-efficacy.

- **Substance abuse**
  Drug abuse jeopardizes our ability to be resilient. This is a highly maladaptive coping strategy.

- **Using instrumental support**
  You accept tangible help from other people, for example help with transport, childcare, housework etc.

- **Venting**
  Angry outbursts, punching of pillows, confronting perceived perpetrators, letting off steam – some see this as helpful, while others believe it merely feeds the flame.

- **Denial**
  Avoidance of facts, denial of the reality of tragic experience is generally counterproductive.

- **Self-blame**
  This is a destructive behaviour, a cognitive process whereby an individual attributes difficult events and stressful occasions in a pattern of self-blame.

Receiving feedback

There are lots of instructions about how to give feedback, but less emphasis on the manner in which we should receive feedback. This can be a vital skill, particularly when we are working on developing our resilience reserves.

1 **Am I ready to receive this feedback?**
Giving permission to the person delivering the message is an important psychic and physical stage in the feedback process. It allows you to open yourself to the message and prepare to listen.

2 **Do I understand the behaviour that is being identified?**
Is this feedback about behaviour that I recognize in myself? Can I recall the event/is this something that is in my memory?

3 **Can I separate the specific issue from my sense of self?**
Listen to the feedback. Can this be heard in a neutral sense? This communication is subjective, it is about something specific. Can I hear this without globally attacking myself as a person? If I do take it this way, I need to recognize that I am being self-destructive.

4 **Do I need to ask any questions for clarification?**
Is there more I want to know? Asking for examples or for the message to be delivered in a way that is clearer to understand is OK. The feedback is only constructive if I have understood what the issue is.

5 **What can I do about this feedback in a constructive way?**
How can I act on this information? What steps can I take to learn from this and how can the person who gave me the feedback support me? Who else is there that might be able to help?

6 **How have I reacted to the feedback?**
Take a few minutes to review your reaction to this feedback. Were you able to listen without distracting emotion? If you did feel angry, upset or distressed, can you locate the reason for that emotional response? Have you been able to take the feedback on board and will you consider it in future scenarios?

Giving upwards feedback

Ideally, managers will be giving regular feedback to those who work for them – this modelling of how to communicate will encourage those that work for you to develop these skills themselves. You can, to this end, encourage upwards feedback. Make it known that as a manager/leader, you are open to hearing people's views and opinions, and developing a culture of open feedback. The qualities of listening, understanding and support are equally valid for leaders and followers.

How you have been and how you will be

When we are challenged 'we are challenged to change ourselves', as stated by Victor Frankl. The choice we have is the choice of our attitude; that is always in our power. If you have struggled with something in the past and responded in a way that is detrimental to your well-being and your self-esteem, you have a choice. You do not have to act in the same way again. People perhaps get used to you being a certain way – particularly accommodating, or short-tempered, or hard to please, for example. This then becomes an expectation – but you can change this. You can make a statement along the lines of: 'I used to find feedback that was not 100 per cent positive very hard to hear. I now realize how valuable that feedback might be and will respond differently in the future.'

1 What is your statement of change?

2 What do you declare about how you will be?

3 Write down and date your statement.

4 Diarize to revisit it and check your progress.

5 How would we deal with this if it were a beloved friend or treasured colleague?

Resilience reassessment

At the start of this book you were invited to undertake a resilience self-assessment. Take the assessment again now – has your resilience developed as a result of your increased understanding and exploration?

Resilience self-assessment

When exploring our resilience, there is often a disparity between our own sense of resilience and the way others see us. It could be that we feel far frailer than we are seen to be... or perhaps because we are quiet, we might be judged as being less resilient. The situations in which we find ourselves can also vary greatly, as, too, can our resilience in these circumstances.

Thinking about yourself at work, how would you rate your sense of resilience? Award yourself a mark out of 10, where 10 is the most resilient. And how would others rate you? Ask a few people (suggestions in the exercise below) to give you a mark out of 10. There is no right or wrong response to the questions posed; the intention of the exercise is to get you to pause and examine yourself a little closer. On a scale of 1 to 10:

- How would you rate yourself?
- How would your partner rate you?
- How would your colleague rate you?
- How would your mentor/coach (if you have one) rate you?
- How would your direct manager rate you?
- How would your friend rate you?

Look at these marks and consider what this might mean. Is there a disparity?

Note: In exploring your self-assessment and the way in which you imagine others see you, it might be worth considering how optimistic or pessimistic you feel you are as a person. Consider how you have behaved when you have had setbacks. Do you find it easy to let go and then carry on, or do these setbacks tend to stay with you?

Endnotes

1 Orwell, G (1937) *The Road to Wigan Pier*, Penguin Modern Classics, London

2 Seligman, M (1972) Learned helplessness, *Annual Review of Medicine*, **23**, pp 407–12, annualreviews.org (archived at https://perma.cc/GLP8-TCBZ)

3 Seligman, M (1990) *Learned Optimism: How to change your mind and your life*, Vintage (Random House), London

4 Sandberg, S and Grant, A (2017) *Option B: Facing adversity, building resilience and finding joy*, W H Allen (Penguin), London

5 Brown, B (2018) *Dare to Lead: Brave work. Tough conversations. Whole hearts*, Penguin, London

6 Day, E (2019) *How to Fail: Everything I've ever learned from things going wrong*, 4th Estate, London

7 Patterson, C (2018) *The Art of Not Falling Apart*, Atlantic Books, London

8 Obama, M (2018) *Becoming*, Crown Publishing Group (Penguin), New York

9 Sandberg, S and Grant, A (2017) *Option B: Facing Adversity, building resilience and finding joy*, W H Allen (Penguin), London

10 Murray, C and Hernstein, R (1994) *The Bell Curve: Intelligence and class structure in American life*, Free Press, New York

11 Gladwell, M (2008) *Outliers: The story of success*, Allen Lane (Penguin), London

12 Duckworth, A (2017) *Grit: Why passion and resilience are the secrets to success*, Vermillion (Penguin), London

13 Garmezy, N, Masten, A, and Best, K, (1990) Resilience and development: Contributions from the study of children who overcome adversity, *Development and Psychopathology*, **2** (4), pp 425–44, doi:10.1017/ S0954579400005812; Garmezy, N (1993) Children in poverty: Resilience despite risk, *Psychiatry*, **56** (1), pp 127–36, doi:10.1080/0033 2747.1993.11024627; Garmezy, N and Cicchetti, D (1993) Prospects and promises in the study of resilience, *Development and Psychopathology*, 5 (4), pp 497–502, doi:10.1017/S0954579400006118

14 Coutu, D (May 2002) How resilience works, *Harvard Business Review*, **80** (5)

15 Coutu, D (May 2002) How resilience works, *Harvard Business Review*, **80** (5)

16 Maya Shankar: From Juilliard to the White House, NPR broadcast, https://www.npr.org/2018/12/28/680679054/loss-and-renewal-moving-forward-after-a-door-closes (archived at https://perma.cc/ LP3T-LMKP)

17 https://www.thefailureinstitute.com (archived at https://perma. cc/87LD-JWXK)

18 Coutu, D (May 2002) How resilience works, *Harvard Business Review*, **80** (5)

19 Greitens, E (2015) *Resilience: Hard-won wisdom for living a better life*, Mariner Books, Boston, New York

20 Cyrulnik, B (2005) *The Whispering of Ghosts: Trauma and resilience*, Other Press, New York

21 Chatterjee, R (2017) *The 4 Pillar Plan: How to relax, eat, move, sleep your way to a longer, healthier life*, Penguin, London; *The Stress Solution: 4 steps to a calmer, happier, healthier you*, Penguin, London, https://drchatterjee.com/blog/category/podcast/ (archived at https://perma.cc/3W2K-38Q6)

BIBLIOGRAPHY

Beer, J E and Stief, E (1997) *The Mediator's Handbook*, revised and expanded third edition, New Society Publishers, Canada

Bion, W R (1959) Attacks on linking, *International Journal of Psychoanalysis*, **40**, pp 308–15

Blasko, D G (1999) Only the tip of the iceberg: Who understands what about metaphor? *Journal of Pragmatics*, **31** (12), pp 1675–83

Brown, B (2015) *Daring Greatly: How the courage to be vulnerable transforms the way we live, love, parent and lead*, Penguin, London

Cain, S (2012) *Quiet: The power of introverts in a world that can't stop talking*, Penguin, London

Chatterjee, R (2017) *The 4 Pillar Plan: How to relax, eat, move, sleep your way to a longer, healthier life*, Penguin, London

Cherry, K (2018) *Sublimation in Behavioral Psychology*, www.verywellmind.com/4172222 (archived at https://perma.cc/J2DA-PMT9)

Cohen, W A (2016) *Peter Drucker on Consulting: How to apply Drucker's principles for business success*, LID Publishing, London

Corrigan, P W, Larson, J E and Ruesch, N (2009) Self-stigma and the 'why try' effect: impact on life goals and evidence-based practices, *World Psychiatry*, **8** (2), pp 75–81

Coutu, D (May 2002) How Resilience Works, *Harvard Business Review*, **80** (5)

Covey, S R, Merrill A R, Merrill R R (1995) *First Things First*, Simon and Schuster, New York

Critchlow, H (2019) *The Science of Fate: Why your future is more predictable than you think*, Hodder & Stoughton, London

Crockett, E & Neff, L A (2013) When receiving help hurts: gender differences in cortisol responses to spousal support, *Social Psychological and Personality Science*, **4** (2), pp 190–97, doi:10.1177/1948550612451621

Csikszentmihalyi, M (1992) *'Flow': The psychology of happiness*, Rider, London

Csikszentmihalyi, M (2003) *Good Business: Leadership flow and the making of meaning*, Viking Penguin, London

Cyrulnik, B (2005) *The Whispering of Ghosts: Trauma and resilience*, Other Press, New York

Cyrulnik, B (2011) *Resilience: How your inner strength can set you free from the past*, Penguin, London

Day, E (2019) *How to Fail: Everything I've ever learned from things going wrong*, Fourth Estate, London

De Dreu, C K W (2008) The virtue and vice of workplace conflict: food for (pessimistic) thought, *Journal of Organizational Behavior*, 29 (1), pp 5–18

Doidge, N (2007) *The Brain that Changes Itself: Stories of personal triumph from the frontiers of brain science*, Penguin, London

Draper, D (2018) *Create Space: How to manage time, and find focus, productivity and success*, Profile Books, London

Dryden, W (2010) *10 Steps to Positive Living*, Orient Paperbacks, Delhi

Duckworth, A (2017) *Grit: Why passion and resilience are the secrets to success*, Vermillion (Penguin) London

Dweck, C S (2006) *Mindset: The new psychology of success*, Random House, New York

Dweck, C S (2012) *Mindset: How you can fulfill your potential*, Constable & Robinson, London

Einarsen, S, Hoel, H, Zapf, D, Cooper, C (2003) *Bullying and Emotional Abuse in the Workplace: International perspectives in research and practice*, CRC Press, Boca Raton, FL

Fisher, R & Ury, W (1981) *Getting to Yes: Negotiating an agreement without giving in*, Random House Business Books, London

Frankl, V (1959) *Man's Search for Meaning*, Rider, London

Freud, A (1937, 1966) *The Ego and the Mechanisms of Defence*, Karnac, London

Freud, S (1917) Mourning and melancholia, *Standard Edition* (vol 14), Hogarth Press, London, also Penguin Modern Classics, London

Garmezy, N (1993) Children in Poverty: resilience despite risk, *Psychiatry*, 56 (1), pp 127–36, doi:10.1080/00332747.1993.11024627

Garmezy, N and Cicchetti, D (1993) Prospects and promises in the study of resilience, *Development and Psychopathology*, 5 (4), pp 497–502, doi:10.1017/S0954579400006118

Garmezy, N, Masten, A, and Best, K (1990) Resilience and development: contributions from the study of children who overcome adversity, *Development and Psychopathology*, 2 (4), pp 425–44, doi:10.1017/S0954579400005812

Giles, S (2018) *The New Science of Radical Innovation*, BenBella Books, Dallas, Texas

Gladwell, M (2008) *Outliers: The story of success*, Allen Lane (Penguin), London

Graham, L (2013) *Bouncing Back: Rewiring your brain for maximum resilience and well-being*, New World Library, Novato, CA

Grant, A (2013) Rethinking the extraverted sales ideal: the ambivert advantage, *Psychological Science*, doi:10.1177/0956797612463706

Grant, A M (2013) *Give and Take: A revolutionary approach to success*, Penguin, London

Grant, A, Gino, F, Hofmann, D A (2011) Reversing the extraverted leadership advantage: the role of employee proactivity, *Academy of Management Journal*, **54** (3), pp 528–50

Greitens, E (2015) *Resilience: Hard-won wisdom for living a better life*, Mariner Books, Boston, New York

Hanson, R (2018) *Resilient: Find your inner strength*, Penguin, London

Harlow, H F and Zimmerman, R (1959) Affectional responses in the infant monkey, *Science*, **130**, pp 421–32

Harvard Business Review (January 5, 2015), quoting Bond and Shapiro's study, *What Resilience Means, and Why It Matters*, Andrea Ovans

Harvard Business Review (February 11, 2016), quoting Emmy Werner

ISPSO, International Society for the Psychoanalytic Study of Organizations, www.ispso.org (archived at https://perma.cc/8K77-SSTG)

Kahn, S (2017) *Death and the City: On Loss, mourning, and melancholia at work*, Karnac, London

Kahneman, D (2011) *Thinking, Fast and Slow*, Allen Lane (Penguin), London

Kirk, J & Wall, C (2010) Resilience and loss in work identities: a narrative analysis of some retired teachers' work-life histories, *British Educational Research Journal*, **36** (10), pp 627–41

Liefooghe, A P D and Mackenzie Davey, K (2010) The language and organization of bullying at work, *Administrative Theory & Praxis*, **32**, pp 71–95

Marsh, H (2014) *Do No Harm: Stories of life, death and brain surgery*, Weidenfeld & Nicolson, London

Murray, C and Hernstein, R (1994) *The Bell Curve: Intelligence and class structure in American life*, Free Press, New York

Neff, K (2003) *Self Compassion: Stop beating yourself up and leave insecurity behind*, Harper Collins, New York

Nietzsche, F (1888/1998) *Twilight of the Idols, on Maxims and Arrows*, Oxford World's Classics, Oxford University Press, Oxford

Oade, A (2015) *Free Yourself from Workplace Bullying: Become bully-proof and regain control of your life*, Mint Hall Publishing, Oxford

Obama, M (2018) *Becoming*, Crown Publishing Group, New York

Obholzer, A and Roberts, V Z (2019) *The Unconscious at Work: A Tavistock approach to making sense of organizational life*, second edition, Karnac, London

Orwell, G (1937) *The Road to Wigan Pier*, Penguin Modern Classics, London

Patterson, C (2018) *The Art of Not Falling Apart*, Atlantic Books, London

Pemberton, C (2015) *Resilience: A practice guide for coaches*, Oxford University Press, Oxford

Quine, C (2006) Discovering purpose: exploring organizational meaning, Grubb Institute working note published in *The Unconscious at Work* (vol 2), Karnac, London

Riggio, R E, Chaleff, I, Lipman-Blumen, J (2008) *The Art of Followership*, Wiley, Hoboken, NJ

Russell, H (2016) *The Year of Living Danishly*, Icon, London

Russell, H (2018) *The Atlas of Happiness: The global secrets of how to be happy*, Hodder & Stoughton, London

Sandberg, S and Grant, A (2017) *Option B: Facing adversity, building resilience and finding joy*, W H Allen (Penguin), London

Sandler, C (2011) *Executive Coaching: A psychodynamic approach*, Open University Press, London

Seligman, M (1972) Learned helplessness, *Annual Review of Medicine*, 23, pp 407–12, www.annualreviews.org (archived at https://perma.cc/UD4T-8K8K)

Seligman M (1990) *Learned Optimism: How to change your mind and your life*, Vintage (Random House), London

Seligman, M (2003) *Authentic Happiness: Using the new positive psychology to realize your potential for lasting fulfilment*, Nicholas Brealey Publishing, London

Seligman, M (2010) *Flourish: Positive psychology and positive interventions*, The Tanner Lectures on Human Values, delivered at The University of Michigan

Seligman, M, Peterson and C, Maier, S F (1993) *Learned Helplessness: A theory for the age of personal control*, Oxford University Press, Oxford

Maya Shankar: From Juilliard to the White House, NPR broadcast, https://www.npr.org/2018/12/28/680679054/loss-and-renewal-moving-forward-after-a-door-closes (archived at https://perma.cc/LP3T-LMKP)

Sinek, S (2009) *Start with Why: How great leaders inspire everyone to take action*, Penguin, London

Skogstad, A, Einarsen, S, Torsheim, T A, Merethe, S and Hetland, H (2007) The destructiveness of laissez-faire leadership behavior, *Journal of Occupational Health Psychology*, **12** (1), pp 80–92

Sostrin, J (2015) *The Manager's Dilemma: Balancing the inverse equation of increasing demands and shrinking resources*, Palgrave Macmillan, London

Spector, P E and Bruk-Lee, V (2008) *Conflict, health, and well-being*, https://my.apa.org (archived at https://perma.cc/9GLK-4TD4)

Storoni, M (2019) *Stress Proof: The ultimate guide to living a stress-free life*, Hodder & Stoughton, London

Stylist Magazine (2018) *Life Lessons from Remarkable Women: Tales of triumph, failure & learning to love yourself*, featuring Bobbi Brown, Penguin Life, London

Tedeschi, R G and Calhoun, L G J (1996) The post-traumatic growth inventory: measuring the positive legacy of trauma, *Journal of Traumatic Stress*, **9** (3), pp 455–71, doi:10.1007/BF02103658

Van Heugten, K (March, 2013) Resilience as an underexplored outcome of workplace bullying, *Qualitative Health Research*, **23** (3), pp 291–301, doi:10.1177/1049732312468251

Wagnild, G (2009) A review of the resilience scale, *Journal of Nursing Measurement*, **17** (2), pp 105–13, doi:10.1891/1061-3749.17.2.105

Waitley, D (1997) *The Psychology of Motivation*, Nightingale-Conant, Wheeling, IL

Walker, M (2017) *Why We Sleep*, Penguin, London

Weber, M (2002) *The Protestant Ethic and the 'Spirit' of Capitalism*, trans P Baehr and G C Wells, Penguin, London

White, S (2013) *The Psychodynamics of Workplace Bullying*, Karnac, London

Winfrey, O (2019) *The Path Made Clear: Discovering your life's direction and purpose*, Bluebird, London

Winnicott, D W (1975) *Through Pediatrics to Psychoanalysis: The collected papers of D W Winnicott*, Basic, New York

Worthington, E L Jr & Scherer, M (2002) Forgiveness is an emotion-focused coping strategy that can reduce health risks and promote health resilience: theory, review, and hypotheses, *Psychology and Health*, **19** (3), pp 385–405, doi:10.1080/0887044042000196674

Websites

https://www.acas.org.uk/index.aspx?articleid=1218 (archived at https://perma.cc/EVK2-D3N3), *Advisory Booklet – Managing conflict at work*

https://www.thebookoflife.com (archived athttps://perma.cc/ET4N-XQC9)

https://www.thefailureinstitute.com (archived athttps://perma.cc/87LD-JWXK)

National Bullying Helpline:
https://www.nationalbullyinghelpline.co.uk (archived at https://perma.cc/F8EB-622B). Workplace-bullying and harassment-disputes specialists that offer employees practical solutions and support. If you require help and advice with bullying at work and don't find the answers to your questions on our website, please call us on 0845 22 55 787

https://www.theschooloflife.com (archived at https://perma.cc/S6CM-EEMT)

https://www.verywellmind.com/practice-focused-meditation-3144785 (archived at https://perma.cc/2RQN-UGRA), *How to Get Started with a Focused Meditation Practice*

INDEX